NO MASK
REQUIRED

NO MASK REQUIRED

HAVE YOU GOT THE FACE TO BE A CHRISTIAN?

A challenge to young people setting out
on the Christian adventure.

MIKE STICKLAND

AUTUMN
HOUSE

Dedication
To Gudrun and John, Felicity and Austin,
Jeni and Nigel, and the many other young
adults with whom I have had the privilege
of sharing the ministry of the Gospel.

'The Christian life is dynamically full and
exciting when you take it on as a full-time,
twenty-four-hours-a-day adventure. There
is never a dull moment in the real cut and
thrust of committed daily living . . . . '

ISBN 1 873796 55 2

Published by
Autumn House
Alma Park, Grantham, Lincolnshire,
NG31 9SL, England

About the author . . .

When Mike Stickland published *Life is an Austin 7: Coping with Cancer and Chemo* (Autumn House) in June 1994, many probably assumed that it would be his last book. It was the story of his long struggle with cancer. Now Mike, a trained youth minister, has written a book targeted directly at young people. Most of his twenty-five-year ministry has been with young people. His ministry has brought many to Christ.

Mike lives in Nottingham with his wife Sheila. They have three sons, Nathan, Bob and Danny.

What's it all about?

Is Christianity a matter of building up a credit of Brownie points?

What are the claims of Jesus?

God wants to save us; but how does His system work? How much of it is down to human grit, and how much to God's own power?

Is the Gospel too good to be true, or too good *not* to be true?

How can we take practical measures to steer our lives away from the pot-holes?

'We can make a list of behaviours unacceptable in a Christian,' writes Mike Stickland. 'Then we can brace ourselves and live up to our list with a little effort. But that's *not* what being a Christian is about. The items on our list are just symptoms of a fundamentally flawed nature we cannot *begin* to remedy . . . .

'You and I are wasting our time trying to be holy by willpower. But there are tasks of which we are capable, and upon which the process of growth is dependent . . . .'

So, have *you* got the face to be a Christian?

Read and find out.

Credits: Biblical quotations are from the New International Version, published by Hodder & Stoughton, unless otherwise stated.

Those marked 'Barclay' are quoted from *The New Testament — A new translation*, by Professor William Barclay, published in two volumes in 1968 by Collins.

Those marked 'The Message New Testament' are quoted from *The Message — A New Testament In Contemporary Language*, by Eugene H. Peterson, published by NavPress in 1993.

Those marked 'J. B. Phillips' are quoted from *The New Testament in Modern English* by J. B. Phillips, published by Collins.

Those marked 'Living Bible' are quoted from *The Living Bible* by Kenneth Taylor, published by Hodder & Stoughton.

Those marked 'Good News Bible' are quoted from *Good News Bible — Today's English Version*, published by the Bible Societies/Collins/Fontana.

NO MASK REQUIRED

Contents

Introduction

AUSTIN AND FELICITY came to visit Sheila and me one Friday evening, and we got talking about what it means to be a Christian. In the course of our conversation we talked about the various 'masks' we wear in daily living, concealing the worst aspects of our characters so that others are impressed by us or simply accept us as colleagues and friends. Such concealment is not cunning deception in any calculated way, but quite normal behaviour in the attempt to survive and to be affirmed. But then we talked about the folly of extending that mask-wearing in our contact with God, because in God's case we fool no one but ourselves. Austin remarked, 'You ought to write this into a book.' This volume is the product of that suggestion.

For most of my years of ministry I have been involved with youth, and much of the material I have written here was first presented at youth retreats, youth camps, or youth days. Some chapters were first presented as several small talks in a series, while other chapters were complete talks which, with others, comprised a whole series. In the process of writing them down I found that what 'carries' in a face-to-face verbal presentation is more difficult to convey, successfully, in a written form; so I have field-tested some elements of the book on youth groups such as in a squash meeting of young people in Grantham, and a young people's Bible study group which my eldest son attends in Watford. I know that young people these days do not read many books from cover to cover, but I hope the lighter, more dynamic portions of this book will help them through the heavier chapters.

I have attempted to make the book appealing and meaningful to young people, but I hope that it will also prove helpful to readers of all ages. One of the saddest people I have met was a man of 72 who had been a Christian since his teens yet had not grasped the peace and wealth of the life the Gospel promises. It is a delight to know God and the peace He offers and, I hope, by reading this volume, you may intensify your trust in Him and be drawn to love Him more deeply.

MIKE STICKLAND

Barking up the wrong bell tower

'LET'S HEAD FOR the church first and do that, then we can relax,' suggested Bob.

'No, let's find the village shop first and stoke up on drinks and snacks. I could do with a bar of the chocolate that helps me "work, rest and play".' That was my preference.

Ever pragmatic, Rick said, 'Let's just hit the village and if we find the shop first we'll stop for snacks, otherwise we'll head for the church.'

The three of us were police cadets with the Norfolk Constabulary. Coming up towards our eighteenth birthdays, we were on the brink of completing the requirements for our 'Silver' in the Duke of Edinburgh's Award Scheme, and were part way through day two of a three-day 'exploration' that was to involve two nights under canvas and a hike of at least thirty miles.

We ambled into the West Norfolk village, backs weary from the weight of packs, feet sore and blistered from hiking some twelve miles that day, and not looking forward to the remaining five miles we had to cover before we pitched camp and awaited a visit from our adjudicator. But it was not just a matter of trudging thirty miles over three days. It was more a matter of demonstrating the ability to map-read, to navigate, to manage ourselves properly over such a venture, and to include some exploration project. In our case Bob, as leader of the group, had decided our project was to visit and report on the churches of the villages through which we were to pass.

To my relief the shop appeared first, and we rested for ten minutes as we downed a can of drink and demolished at least one Mars bar each. Suitably replenished, we made for the church that stood across a neat village green opposite a row of cottages. Initially we wandered around the churchyard, looking for interesting gravestones, then found that the church door was open, as they usually were back in the early 1960s; so we continued our investigation inside. At the bookstand we picked up an information leaflet which we used to guide ourselves round the major features of the building, and then found that the door to the belfry was also unlocked. We could not resist climbing up the system of ladders until we were adjacent to the bell.

Being the most serious of the three, Bob started to make notes about the bell: its size, the method of fixing to its axis, and the foundry in which it had been cast.

Being the least serious of the bunch, I decided it would be well to discover something of the tone of the bell. Being mischievous too, I recalled hearing somewhere that it was not possible to remain standing immediately beside a bell as it tolled, and that the shock waves and sheer volume could make you fall to your knees. I could take great delight in seeing Rick and Bob fall to their knees! So I scooted back down the ladders until I was at a safe distance, and at a place where I hoped I could brace myself against such indignity, and then I pulled my weight on the rope.

The huge bell swung to life with a sound that resonated through my head. It did not cause my mates to fall over, but it did bring the church warden scurrying across the green to see who was messing about in the church. It was not easy to convince him that rather than being hooligans or vandals we were respectable police cadets out on an equally respectable task associated with the Duke of Edinburgh's Award. We trembled in our boots for a while, but fortunately for us he eventually laughed it off and we went on our way, relieved that he was not going to report us.

In another time and at another place, John Bunyan stood in fear of the consequences of ringing the church bells. Like me, Bunyan had a fascination for bells, except that generally he rang them *with* the approval of the church warden. He had nothing to fear from him! Indeed, John's problem was not directly with human beings at all, it was with God!

Even as a child of 9, John was troubled by the most awful nightmares in which he imagined God's pursuing him and punishing him. He was terrified that his destiny was hell-fire. The constant rebuke of the village parson and the fire and fear within the parson's sermons led John to conclude that he was riddled with sin — and was thus beyond redemption. He had it all worked out. Looking back on that period of his life he felt compelled to conclude that he had become *'the very ringleader of all the village youth in all manner of vice and ungodliness'.*[1]

For a while in his teens, John ignored his fear of God, deciding more or less to indulge in as wild a time as possible, because if God was inevitably going to get him, he might as well enjoy life meanwhile. He persistently used profanities in his conversation, so that it made people recoil from his presence. He used to drink a lot and was often very drunk. He liked to join the other village youth in a wild game of tipcat on Sundays. And he liked to ring the church bells — not bad in itself, but in those days pleasure of any kind was deemed sinful.

It was the influence of his young wife, and her threat to leave him, that brought John up with a start when he was about 20, and he decided to try to live a godly life. Mostly he did that by reforming his outward behaviour. He started attending church twice each Sunday, stopped his swearing, stopped drinking alcohol, stopped his Sunday games of tipcat, and kept completely away from the bell tower, where he thought God's wrath could easily be unleashed by the bell's falling from its beam and crushing him below!

Although he did not realize it at the time, poor John was barking up the wrong bell tower. He thought that by action limited to modifying his standards and revising his behaviour he could gain forgiveness and approval from God and man. His neighbours certainly praised him for his reformed character, and that made him feel good, but in time he was to recognize that he could not fool God and nor could he fool himself. He wrote, *'I was nothing but a poor painted hypocrite, yet I loved to be talked of as one that was truly godly. I was proud of my godliness, and, indeed, I did all I did, either to be seen of, or to be well spoken of, by man. And this I continued for about a twelvemonth or more.'*

In lots of ways, John was just like us. We 'wear masks' in every-day life to conceal what we are really like, because it is important to us that other people like us. In other words, we modify our behaviour according to the circumstances in which we find ourselves, in order to be accepted and receive vital affirmation from others.

I can illustrate this better if I ask you to imagine sitting with me at a dressing-table mirror. We look into the mirror and see reflected the person we really are, 'warts and all', with no frills or falsity — *'The Real Me'* if you like. We see ourselves as only those see us who live in close proximity to us day in and day out, such as our immediate family. It may not be a pretty picture! Unless we are relaxed and have confidence in the people around us, we seldom show this face in public.

As we observe ourselves in that mirror we are also aware that there is a person that we strive to be who is different from the person we actually are. On a very trivial level, this is demonstrated each morning in the bathroom. We wash our face, comb our hair, shave (or not, according to preference), and try to look as presentable as possible. At the same time, especially when we are teenagers, we wish we were more handsome or more beautiful, that we had a better physique or figure, that our hair was more curly or less curly, that it was not turning so grey so early, or receding so fast. We are not quite as perfect as we would wish, so we groom ourselves, using clothes, gels and perhaps make-up, to enhance our looks as much as possible

On a more serious level, we also recognize that our characters are not always what they could be. We might wish we were more patient, or perhaps more assertive. We might wish we were not so easily dominated by others, or we might aspire to be more successful than we are, or more intelligent, capable, skilled, 'together' and so on. There is a distinct shortfall between the person we actually are and the person we want to be. I have yet to find a human who does not have some ambition to be different in some respect or another.

Our instinctive remedy is to resort to pretence. Imagine that on the table there are three face masks, each identified by a label. The label on the first mask reads, *The Person I Want to be*, and often when we look into that mirror we fail to see the 'real me', because we have hidden behind this mask. We find it very reassuring and much less threatening to wear this mask rather than face reality.

The label on the second mask reads *The Person that Other People Expect Me to be*, and it acknowledges that everyone living around us has his own expectation of the way we should behave. This varies in different contexts, but generally I think you will find that we are aware of such expectations; we do acknowledge that these expectations may be at variance with the person we actually are, and we try to modify ourselves and our behaviour because we want those around us to accept us. Because one of the strongest motivations known to humans is the need to be accepted and popular, we will often suppress our own preference, or conceal our real selves in order that we may receive such affirmation. We instinctively wear this mask from the moment we step out of our front door each morning.

The third mask is labelled *The Person I Ought to be*, and represents the higher and more noble dimensions of life. If we are religious, it represents the person we feel God wishes us to be. All right, many people do not care much about God or His expectations, but those with even the smallest recognition of God do have a picture in their minds of His expectations of them. Even those who do not consider themselves to be religious have concepts of those deep qualities that are right, dignified and virtuous.

We may have gleaned such concepts from our parents, from church, from a role-model or mentor, or just from life, but we each have a picture, and from experience I would say that picture is different from the person we really *are*; it is different from the person we *want to be*, and it is often in tension with the person we are *expected to be*. Our own ambitions are frequently in conflict with the expectations we believe God has of us. We do not necessarily always want to be that noble! God may want us to 'Go the second mile' or to 'Turn the other cheek', but that is not what we want. We want our independence! So we wear the third mask only occasionally, perhaps when we are trying to impress God or someone from the church!

Let me demonstrate how these masks impinge upon everyday life.

You are job hunting. You keenly want a job that has been advertised in a local solicitors' office. It has good prospects, attractive working conditions and you have heard the salary is good. By nature you like to hang around in trainers, jeans and sweatshirt, but you notice that at this solicitors' office they all wear suits. Even the secretaries and typists wear suits. You don't much like suits and you wouldn't by nature choose to wear one, but you want the job. Do you persist in wearing your trainers and jeans to the interview? No, you concede to the expectations you have perceived they have, and you modify your clothing and your deportment in order to get the job. You may not go out and buy a suit yet, but you decide to wear your best combination of clothes. You have opted to be something other than your real self, because you recognize it is in your own interests to do so. You are going to 'wear a mask' to give the impression this is the real you.

Or suppose you now have the job, and have been invited out tenpin bowling with all your mates. The only time the lanes are available is one hour after work, so you agree you will all converge on The Alley from your own places of work and study. You will have insufficient time to get home to change out of your suit and into your Levis. Do you plan to remain in your office suit or do you take a bag with your jeans and Michael Jordan T-shirt and trainers in it, to change quickly once you arrive at The Alley? I think you take your spare clothes with you, because you wouldn't be seen dead dressed up in a suit unless you happen to learn that they are all going in their suits too. You have chosen to drop the version of Mask No. 2 you have worn at work, and wear a revised version for the evening. You will be a little bit more yourself, but only so far as peer pressure will allow.

Or you are going to meet the parents of your boy-friend/girl-friend for the first time. You have the feeling his/her dad is not sure about you yet, so you are keen to make a good impression. You hate washing up, but you learn from your boy-friend/girl-friend that you will be expected to get out and help with the dishes since Mum will have been at work all day. Do you stand on your dignity and insist on lounging in front of the TV while the others do the dishes (after all, you *are* the guest!)? Or do you roll up your sleeves in the interests of getting another invitation and gaining approval of your friendship with their son/daughter? You are very much back in a mask, doing something that doesn't come naturally, so as to impress.

Now suppose that the local pastor is coming to your home tonight at your request, to talk about your decision to be a Christian and be baptized. How would you speak to him? How would you dress? How would you relate to your annoying kid brother while the pastor was around on that visit? I suggest that you may well 'wear a mask' pretty close to mask No. 3, because in the back of your mind the pastor represents God, and somewhere inside you want to appear as much like a godly person as possible.

Now for the crunch as we extend this procedure, and apply it to the human struggle to satisfy God! We are obliged to concede that we play the mask game as we interface with each other. What may be more difficult to recognize is an instinctive tendency to resort to the same deception as we interface with God.

When John Bunyan stopped drinking at the alehouse, what was he doing? When he stopped his swearing, dancing, playing tipcat and ringing the church bells, what was he doing? Was he not acknowledging the same principles of the three masks that we have just acknowledged? Was he not admitting that the real John Bunyan was not the John Bunyan that he deeply wanted to be, nor the John Bunyan that other people expected him to be? He was resorting to superficial changes and to mask-wearing.

When John stopped his drinking, he did so because he wanted to be acceptable to his wife. When he stopped his swearing, he did so because he was ashamed to be known as the 'vilest' young man in the village and he wanted to change that. When he stopped joining the country dancing, and stopped playing tipcat on the Sabbath, and stopped ringing the church bells that had given him so much pleasure, all he was doing was attempting to conform to the expectations he had learned others had of him, whether those "others" were human or divine.

Because he succeeded in convincing his neighbours, for a while he thought he could also convince God. He was trying to satisfy all of God's requirements by modifying his behaviour, and although he would have claimed the change was quite radical and thorough, it was actually quite superficial. At worst he was trying to conceal the truth by pretence. At best he was trying to forge himself into the person represented by mask three, thinking that that was what God expected. This enabled him to overlook the past of the real John Bunyan and to ignore the futility of his persistent failure in the present. Did this reform bring him peace of mind or bring long-term reassurance that he had satisfied God? No!

It was the chance overhearing of some pauper women talking in Bedford that drove this point home, and began to wake John up to something better. The women sat in the sun talking about their faith, about the work of God in their lives. They spoke with such joy and delight that it seemed to John they *'had found a new world'*. He was so taken by their obvious joy and peace that he went over and spoke with them, returning on many an occasion after that to hear more. They introduced him to Pastor John Gifford who, in turn, introduced him to the possibility of God's gracious forgiveness, available by receiving Jesus as his personal Saviour.

There continued an immense struggle within John's mind, and for weeks at a time he wallowed in dejection as he lost hope of ever finding peace and assurance. But eventually he found a rich peace with God, based upon a radical dependence upon what God had to offer him instead of what he had to offer God.

And what of you and me? There is an instinctive tendency to follow the same route that John Bunyan tried. Because we are so accustomed to playing the mask game in our social interaction with each other, it comes fairly naturally to resort to the same technique as we attempt to interact with God.

Imagine yourself in a room in which there are four chairs, marked in the same way as the masks above. Chair one is marked *'The Real Me'*; chair two is marked *'The Person I Want to be'*; chair three is marked *'The Person Others Expect Me to be'*; and chair four is marked *'The Person God wants*

Me to be'. Your purpose in the room is to encounter God.

Imagine that room to be any spot where you feel you can approach God undisturbed and uninterrupted to find peace and forgiveness with Him, whether that be a church building or your own bedroom. You are alone, and you need not impress any other human being. What chair must you sit in, so to speak, or what attitude must you adopt in your prayer, in order that God may recognize and accept you, that He may hear your prayer and extend to you the forgiving disposition that you hope for?

Consider often and with care, the following crucial verses:

'To claim that we have no sin is an act of self-deception, and a proof that we have no idea of the truth. If we confess our sins, we can depend on him, even although he is just, to forgive us our sins, and to purify us from every kind of wickedness. To say that we have never committed a sin is as good as to call him a liar, and to prove that we have no idea what his message means.'[2]

If we transposed that passage into the context of the 'four chairs' illustration, it might then read: 'To sit in Chair four is an act of self-deception, and a proof that we have no idea of the truth. To sit in Chairs two or three is just as much a denial of the truth. But if we sit in Chair one, we can depend on God, even though He is just, to receive and accept us, to forgive us our sins, and to purify us from every kind of wickedness. To pretend that we are something we are not, or that we have achieved all of God's standards is to call Him a liar, and to prove that we have no idea what His message means.'

When we stop and think about it, we recognize the folly of trying to pretend to God that we are something we are not. God sees us exactly as we really are. It is pointless to pretend we are something different. He recognizes only the truth.

'God accepts us just as we are' is more than a useful adage. It is the only basis upon which God will receive us. Jesus said as much in His parable:

'Two men went up to the temple to pray. One was a Pharisee, the other a tax collector. The Pharisee stood there and this was his prayer, and it was addressed quite as much to

himself as it was to God: "O God, I thank you that I am not like other people — rapacious, dishonest, adulterers — or even like this tax-collector here. I fast twice a week. I meticulously set aside for you a tenth of my income." The tax-collector respectfully kept his distance, and would not even look up to heaven. So far from that, he beat his breast and said: "God! Have mercy on me, the sinner!" I tell you, the latter went home far closer to God than the other, for everyone who exalts himself will be humbled, but, if a man humbles himself, he will be received and exalted.[3]

Not only do we have a tendency to resort to mask-wearing in our communication with God; we are inclined also to feel we have to close the gap between 'what we are' and 'what God expects us to be' by our own endeavour. In that sense, too, we align ourselves with John Bunyan, because we find the corresponding gulf between what we believe are the expectations of Christian behaviour and our actual achievement. If our salvation depends upon *our* closing that gap by personal effort, it is enough to make us give up in despondency, as indeed many have.

But we would not be alone in feeling frustrated with ourselves! At times the Apostle Paul experienced the same feelings, and wrote, *'I find it to be a principle of life that, even when I want to do the right thing, the one thing that I can do is the wrong thing . . . . I am a wretched creature. Who will rescue me from this body which turns life into death?'* But then he rejoiced, *'God alone can through Jesus Christ our Lord!'*[4]

It takes 'a lot of bottle', as we say colloquially, to abandon all pretence, to drop all our masks, and to face God the way we are. It takes courage to admit even to ourselves what we are really like and how hopelessly we fail. It takes courage to abandon our own efforts to arrive at our perceived standards. We fear the risk of being rejected. But this is the first essential step to becoming a Christian.

Have you got the bottle?

---

[1]All italicised passages referring to Bunyan in this chapter are quoted from his autobiographical *Grace Abounding*, published by Word (UK) Ltd. [2]1 John 1:8, 9 (Barclay). [3]Luke 18:9-14 (Barclay). [4]Romans 7:21, 24 (Barclay).

The 'Brownie point' fallacy

ONE OF OUR most compelling needs is to be accepted. We crave approval for who we are and praise for what we do. I need you to accept me and to like me. You need me to accept and like you. Such endorsement creates confidence in our inner selves that we have value and are loved. If we are constantly rejected, if we seldom experience affirmation, then we crumble inside; we become more and more insecure, and we may even conclude that we are worthless and unloved. The world is full of people who resort to awful actions as a result of feeling unloved.

We have instinctive protection devices to avoid the hurt of possible rejection, one of which is the subconscious wearing of masks which we noticed in the preceding chapter. As someone has said, 'I am afraid to tell you who I am, because if I tell you who I am, you may not like who I am, and it's all that I have!' It is just too hazardous to risk being rejected or made to feel irrelevant or peculiar.

We learn this lesson very early in life. Survival on the school playground depends on it. We dread being isolated by our peers because we are too fat or too thin, too tall or too short. We hate being the 'odd one out' in any respect because it exposes us to ridicule. We wither each time we are embarrassed in the classroom or on the games field. We fear being shamed in front of our friends, and we will do almost anything to 'keep up appearances'.

However, in this chapter I wish to look at a variation on that theme. Before we ever start school, we begin to learn from the reactions we get at home. Because we crave acceptance and approval, we enjoy the 'warm fuzzy feeling' we get when Mum gives us a hug and thanks us for fulfilling a chore. We respond to the message: 'Mummy loves you when you tidy your room,' and we are likely to repeat the duty just to get some more cuddles. It feels nice when Dad sits us on his knee and says, 'I love you, Son. Thank you for helping me cut the grass.' We enjoy the reassurance of receiving praise and appreciation. But there is a negative risk. We begin to associate warmth and love with the satisfactory completion of good deeds. The system of motivation-by-praise begins to instil into our subconscious the concept that perhaps Mummy and Daddy do *not* love us if we do not deliver some benefit to them.

This risk is reinforced when Mum and Dad seem indifferent to us when we behave neutrally, especially if we have siblings who seem to get praise and affection when we do not. It is further reinforced when we misbehave and are punished, because the sanctions of punishment make us feel exposed and rejected. A minor rebuke which was not intended to threaten us seriously can actually intensify our insecurity. Suppose Mum says, 'Daddy doesn't love you when you scribble on the wall' or Dad says, 'Mummy won't think much of you when she sees you've emptied her talcum powder all over the bathroom', how does that affect us? Maybe not at all if it happens only once, but repeated over our infancy it begins to teach us that we cannot get on in life and we will not receive essential affirmation unless we can accumulate some 'Brownie points'.

This is not to suggest, even remotely, that parents should not stimulate or motivate their children by praise and affection, nor that they should never punish or rebuke their infants. Both are indispensable to produce a balanced young adult in due course. What would be better avoided is giving the impression that we are loved *only* when we deliver some benefit, or that we are *not* loved at all when we behave neutrally or badly. Even in punishment, we must have the reassurance that we are deeply loved and affirmed. It is vital that we feel secure because we know our parents love us for who we are, not for what we do or resist doing.

This is all bad enough in the context of striving to reach adulthood with some equilibrium to our character, but it does not stop there. Because we form our conception of God from the impression our parents (especially our fathers) make, we are very likely to transfer the 'Brownie point' mentality to our negotiations with God too. If we have perceived that we are accepted and loved only on the basis of positive performance, it is natural to conclude that God will accept us only on that basis, too. It becomes very hard for us to accept conclusively that God welcomes us without personal merit points, if our parents have never reassured us in that way so far as their relationship with us is concerned. We find it almost irresistible to presume that sooner or later we must do something to merit credit in God's eyes.

The simple Bible stories, that we may well have heard many times by the time we reach young-adulthood, seem at first glance to reinforce the 'Brownie point' system. Remember the parable about the wise and foolish builders? The wise man built his house on the rock, while the foolish man built on the sand. When the storms came, the house on the sand was washed away, but the house on the rock stood firm. And the point Jesus was making was that it is not people who merely *hear* His instruction who are safe for eternity, but those who hear *and obey*. Surely that obedience implies some recognition based on performance?

It comes as a shock to those of the Brownie-point mindset, to be confronted with those other words of Jesus, spoken in the same place and on the same day, when He said, *'"Many will say to me on that day, 'Lord, Lord, did we not prophecy in your name, and in your name drive out demons and perform many miracles?' Then I will tell them plainly, 'I never knew you.'"'*[1]

Their argument seems to be, 'Surely we deserve some credit for all the good things we have done, otherwise we wasted our time! Doesn't all our effort count for something?' Jesus' predicted response will be, 'That's right; you wasted your time. I never knew you because simply "doing things" in anticipation of merit or recognition is not what it is all about.'

There is a divine expectation that our lives shall reflect the standards God has set. The Ten Commandments and the pattern established by Jesus' Sermon on the Mount remain the criteria for our lives and provide the definition of sin. But the crucial mistake of humanity, and one which we find it difficult to shake off, is that we expect *reward* when what God offers can in no sense be classified as 'reward'. It is a gift which we do nothing to merit. No such reward is available.

Paul summarized it this way: *'The whole process comes from nothing that we have done or could do; it is God's gift. Any achievement of ours is ruled out!'*[2]

Have you ever puzzled over the experience of Ananias and Sapphira recorded in Acts 5? They were Jewish members of the early Christian church, who owned some property which they decided to sell, just as a number of others had done, to provide for the common interest of all Messianic believers and to assist with the evangelistic thrust of those earliest days of the church. There was an almost euphoric unity among the believers in those first tentative weeks and a deep conviction that Jesus would return very shortly. *'No one,'* it records in Acts, *'claimed that any of his possessions was his own, but they shared everything they had. . . . From time to time those who owned lands or houses sold them, brought the money from the sales and put it at the apostles' feet, and it was distributed to anyone as he had need.'*[3]

Ananias and Sapphira joined those who had sold property, but in their case they chose to bring only a portion of the proceeds to the apostles, pretending that it was 100 per cent of the income from the sale. Peter asked Ananias what had caused him to behave that way. The property was his, and he had the perfect right to retain it, or to sell it and retain all or part of the proceeds, or to sell it and give the whole amount to the church. That was a personal matter, and there was no compulsion, no directive from God or the church.

Ask yourself why some people would decide to sell, and then pretend to surrender the total amount while actually retaining some of the proceeds for themselves. Is it not a matter of seeking approval from the group? Their motivation was the public acknowledgement that was associated with the sacrifice. They wanted the acclaim without the forfeiture. They wanted people to think well of them. They wanted to be perceived as wonderful, totally committed believers who were demonstrably living as God wanted them to live. They were after 'Brownie points'.

Their performance illustrates that other human frailty, pride. We are intensely proud creatures. Not only have we been conditioned to expect reward for doing good things, but we are fiercely conceited about our assumed goodness, and we demand recognition for it. It just isn't fair if we are not given praise, and it cuts to the quick if someone else gets the honour we had thought should rightly be ours.

There is a rather obscure story from the Old Testament that is an apt illustration of the human tendency to expect commendation. Zechariah was a priest and prophet who records a visit to Jerusalem of some Jewish envoys from Babylon. They were sent with an enquiry on behalf of all those Jews who had remained in Babylonia after the release from captivity. They had established 'days of mourning' during which they could express their remorse at what had befallen the city of Jerusalem when Nebuchadnezzar ransacked it. But then, some years after a minority had returned to Jerusalem and word was spreading even to Babylonia that the city was rebuilt and the temple virtually ready to be rededicated, they wished to know whether they might cease commemorating these days of mourning without offending God.

Their egos craved God's approval. They wanted to hear Him say, 'Well done! I acknowledge your devotion and loyalty and commend you for remembering My city so punctiliously all these years by your days of mourning. You have My approval to set these aside now.'

God's actual answer, therefore, came as a deep shock to them, because He said, 'It was not My idea or request that you had days of mourning. That was your own idea! It was My request that you treat each other with dignity, that you do not "ride roughshod" over people; that you do not even think that way, but that you model your lives with moral decency. Now you come expecting Brownie points for something I never even asked of you while you ignore what I did ask you to do! No way!'

I am inclined to think of this Brownie-point mentality as a 'Babylonian' fallacy. Let me explain.

In Genesis 11, the earth is repopulating fast after Noah's flood, and clans and nations of people are migrating and putting down roots in new lands. Those who travelled to the

Land of Shinar, which is the Babylonia of Bible times and roughly equates to modern Iraq, found themselves on fertile plains which promised them a wonderful living, but it also reminded them of the possibility of repeat flooding. They were not prepared to accept God's word that He would never again flood the whole earth, and so they instituted their own contingency plans. They decided to build a tower which would provide them with refuge should God forget, or should He renege on His word, or even prove incapable of controlling the forces of nature. They wanted independence. They didn't trust God; so they wanted a way by which they could ignore or forget Him.

God upset their plans by confusing their language, and the building programme was halted, abandoned in total disarray. But a new cast was set!

• On the one hand there were those of the Babel influence who would do things their own way, independent of God. They would try to make a name for themselves, seek to become a great nation, conquer their neighbours, all according to their own schemes and devices.

• On the other hand was Abraham, who deliberately got away from the Babel influence and moved in the opposite direction by migrating out of Shinar. Abraham's was going to be God's way of life. He simply accepted God's directives and followed them, even when he could see no purpose. When God promised him: *'I will bless you and make your name famous and your descendants will become a great nation'* he *'took God at his word, and that act of faith was accepted as putting him into a right relationship with God.'*

People have tended to segregate themselves along the same demarcation lines ever since. Even religious people can be divided between the two schools of thought. There are those of the Babel mind-set, *'Babylonians'* if you please. And there are those of Abraham's mind-set.

Religious people of the Babylonian disposition tend to depend on their own solutions instead of trusting God's solutions. They carry over the Brownie-point mentality from everyday life into their religious life, and they remain enslaved to the principle that they must accrue merit by their personal good works.

Religious people of the Abrahamic disposition abandon dependence on their own achievements and accept God's way of salvation. *'So then, you are bound to see that it is the people who rely entirely on faith who are sons of Abraham.'*[6] That was the very ethos of the Protestant Reformation, although many Protestants have subsequently reverted to the Babylonian mind-set.

As one observer has written, 'What people desire is a method of forgetting God which will pass as a method of remembering Him.' Does that make sense to you? I think it is a true observation that people want to hang on to their own schemes and devices and yet they want to convince themselves that they are satisfying God. What they settle for is what we have identified above as the *'Babylonian principle'*, so while they never actually surrender to God, they act as if they have and they fool themselves that they have. They build their own version of the Tower of Babel.

The tragedy is that one of the closing passages in the Bible sounds a clarion call to mankind, *'"Babylon has fallen! Come out, my people! Come out from her!"'*[7] The tragedy is not in the message but in the delusion that Babylon has caused. Life has taught us to rely on accruing 'Brownie points' and we have transferred that principle over to our negotiations with God.

It takes a great deal of 'bottle' to abandon what we cling to as our own merits, and come out of Babylon, just as it takes 'bottle' to drop all our masks and face God as we really are. But it is the only way God can release the gift of life to us.

Jesus exposed the fallacy of the 'Brownie point' mentality of the Pharisees when He remarked, *'Tragic will be the fate of you experts in the Law and you Pharisees with your façade of ostentatious piety! For you meticulously pay the tenth part of your crop of mint and dill and cummin to the Temple, and you completely neglect the more important demands of the Law — justice, mercy and loyalty. . . . You are* *like white-washed tombs, which look beautiful from the out-side, but which are full of dead men's bones and all kinds of filth. So you too, as far as external appearances go, seem to people to be carefully obeying the Law, but you are really putting on an act, for inside you are full of disobedience to the Law.*⁸

This is a very hard lesson for us to receive deeply into our hearts. By force of habit and by years of indoctrination, we revert to trusting our own merits. It reminds me of a story related by Lillian Guild:

'While driving on the turnpike in up-State New York one day, we noticed a well-dressed but bewildered man standing alongside a shiny new Cadillac. It was apparent that he was in trouble.

'Since there was room, we pulled over to see if we could be of assistance.

'"What's wrong?" we asked. "Can we help you?"

'"I'm out of gas," he replied. "Of all times for this to happen. I'm late now for an important engagement."

'Fortunately we were carrying a gallon can of gasoline, and my husband emptied it into his tank.

'"You can get gas six miles ahead at the next service area," we told him.

'The man thanked us politely, jumped into his car, and sped away.

'About twelve miles down the road we were astonished to see the same man, with the same car, in the very same pre-dicament! Not wanting to take the time to stop for fuel, he had passed by the service area.'⁹

Trying to run a car without fuel inevitably results in fail-ure. Those who resisted Noah's invitation to board the ark perished in the flood. Those who rely on brownie-point salvation schemes will go down with Babylon just as surely as those who clung on to independent arrangements to survive the Flood, perished.

We must bring ourselves to submit to God's way of doing things. That means we must come to Him for forgive-ness (justification, remedying our past deficiencies) on His terms. It means we must seek cleansing by the process of the

Holy Spirit (sanctification, remedying our present deficiencies) on His terms, too. For 'in the gospel a righteousness from God is revealed, a righteousness that is *by faith from first to last.*'[10]

---

[1]Matthew 7:22, 23. [2]Ephesians 2:8, 9 (Barclay). [3]Acts 4:32ff. [4]See Genesis 12:1-3, Good News. [5]Galatians 3:6 (Barclay). [6]Galatians 3:7 (Barclay). [7]Revelation 18:4, Good News. [8]Matthew 23:23ff. (Barclay). [9]*Ministry* magazine, May 1985. [10]Romans 1:17.

This is the Man!

THE STORY MAY be true; it may be apocryphal, or it may be fifty/fifty and thus a part of the hype.

It revolved around Maurice Saatchi, of Saatchi & Saatchi, the international publicity and advertising agency. Apparently he was on a business visit to one of the large American cities, and was travelling from his hotel to his appointment when he passed a man begging on the pavement. A simple cardboard sign was strung around the beggar's neck with the single word 'BLIND' scrawled on it.

Noticing that people were just passing the man by, not heeding in the least his unspoken appeal for support, Saatchi stopped to talk to him and asked if he could add some words that may stimulate a better response. The man agreed, and in a couple of seconds Saatchi continued on his way.

His business appointment completed, Saatchi returned by the same route and was delighted to see that now the begging-hat was overflowing, which of course he attributed to his additional words, *'AND IT'S SPRING'*. How could those gifted with sight, and the full ability to enjoy springtime, ignore the appeals of one whose appreciation of the season must be somewhat restricted?

Did Jesus need Saatchi? Would a publicity expert have been able to enhance Jesus' success rate in convincing the common man and the Jewish leadership of the authenticity of His credentials? After all, it was His purpose to convince them that He was the Messiah, provided by Yahweh for the salvation of Israel, and yet on the face of it He failed to convince many at all.

The Jewish people were looking for the Messiah to come. The more devout had studied their Scriptures and knew that the time must be near when the Messiah of God would be revealed. The prophet Daniel had specified unambiguously the number of years that would pass between the decree to rebuild the city of Jerusalem after the Jewish captivity in Babylon, and the coming of the 'Anointed One'.[1] That period had just about expired.

Meanwhile the more secular-minded Jews were chaffing

under the rule of Rome, and knew enough of Jewish tradition to hope that a new king of David's line would shortly appear to liberate them. Perhaps they were looking for the wrong kind of 'Messiah', but they were looking. Indeed, there had been a number of times when hopes were raised to fever-pitch, such as during the Second Jewish Revolt led by Simon Bar Kochba. Could he be the Messiah? the people had speculated.

Some of the rabbis began to want to contain such speculation, and suggested pointers by which Messiah could be correctly identified when He did manifest Himself. For example, they had developed a list of major signs, or miracles, by which the true Messiah would reveal Himself and give evidence of His identity. This list was triggered by prophetic passages from Isaiah concerning the coming of Messiah:

— He will make the blind to see (Isaiah 29:18; 35:5)
— He will make the lame walk (Isaiah 35:6)
— He will make the deaf hear (Isaiah 29:18; 35:5)
— He will raise the dead (implied in Isaiah 11:1-2)
— He will evangelize the poor (Isaiah 61:1, 2)

'By the first century Judaism had developed a list of major signs the true Messiah could be expected to give as proof of His identity (see Matt. 16:1-4). Healing a leper was one of them. Another was casting out a deaf, dumb and blind demon (Matt. 12:22, 23). Other Messianic signs and references to them are found in Matt. 11:2-6; John 6:25-33; 9:1-41; 11:1-52.'[2]

Being conscious of this expectation makes a study of the Gospel of John particularly fascinating. After all, John declared that when he wrote his Gospel he had been compelled to be selective of the thousands of miracles Jesus had performed, but had related sufficient to convince any reader that Messiah had come in the Person of Jesus.[3]

Note especially the tension that John records in chapters 7 to 11 when the common people can see that Jesus of Nazareth fulfils all these expectations, and they ask, '"When the Christ comes, will he do more miraculous signs than this man?"' (NIV); *'"When the Messiah comes, . . . surely he will not provide greater demonstrations of the power of God in action than this man has done?"'* (Barclay); *'"What miracles do you expect the Messiah to do that this man has not done?"'* (Living Bible).⁴ In contrast, the Jewish leaders stubbornly resisted such a conclusion: *"Has any of the rulers or of the Pharisees believed in him? No!"'*⁵

It is also interesting to detect that when John the Baptist sent messengers to Jesus with the enquiry, *'"Are you the one who was to come?"'*⁶ a list of the very 'Messiah miracles' enumerated by Isaiah, and scheduled by the rabbis as being the criteria of the true messiah, comprised Jesus' reply. He sends back the message: *'"Go, . . . and tell John the story of all you are hearing and seeing. Blind men are seeing again; lame men are walking; lepers are being cleansed; deaf men are hearing; dead men are being raised to life; poor men are hearing the Good News. And happy is the man who does not find himself antagonised by me."'*⁷

We could look in more detail at the very occurrences to which Jesus has alluded by starting in Luke 5.

*'When Jesus was in one of the towns, a man who was a mass of leprosy came and threw himself prostrate in front of him. "Sir," he appealed to Jesus, "if you want to cure me you can." Jesus reached out his hand and touched him. "I do," he said, "Be cured!" There and then the leprosy left him. Jesus gave him orders not to tell anyone. "Instead, as a testimony to him, go straight to the priest and make an offering for your cleansing as Moses commanded."'*⁸

If a leper who had been healed were to do what the Torah commands he would have to report to the priest. This would send a message to the religious establishment that the Messiah had come and was at work, doing what they knew only Messiah could do. Although Moses had gone to great lengths to outline the appropriate actions for a cured leper to follow — reporting to the priest for a personal physical examination and offering a series of sacrifices — never in the history of Israel had anyone actually had to follow those instructions. No Israelite had ever been cured. Hence the priest's 'testimony' that the leper was clean, was also a 'testimony' that Messiah had come.

The man duly reported to the priest, and the desired effect was achieved. From *'every village of Galilee and from Judea and Jerusalem'*[9] such numbers of Pharisees and teachers of the law appeared that the ordinary folk could not get near Jesus. According to expectation, the rabbis had responded to the cleansed-leper testimony by sending investigators to look into the possibility that Jesus of Nazareth might be Messiah.

The unwritten 'rules of engagement' in such investigations limited initial contact to observation. There was to be no engaging the subject in debate or discussion of their mission, just a quiet, removed scrutiny. The practice can be observed in this evaluation of Jesus and during the similar assessment of the possibility that John the Baptist might have been Messiah. Read through the accounts and you will see that during the first encounters with both the Baptist and Jesus, these 'detectives' did not engage the subject in dialogue, did not question him directly at all, but stood off, making private conclusions. If they found reason to follow the investigation further, then on subsequent reconnoitres it might prove appropriate to engage in dialogue to try to confirm one way or the other what their report to the rabbis should be.

Jesus was aware of the reason for this sudden interest and took the opportunity to demonstrate in another way His claims to be Messiah. When the paralytic was lowered through the roof, Jesus told him, *'"Friend, your sins are forgiven."'*[10] The investigating Pharisees and teachers of the law murmured together in shocked dismay, *'"Who is this fellow who speaks blasphemy? Who can forgive sins but God alone?"'*[11]

And that was exactly the point Jesus was seeking to make. He could forgive sin, because He was Messiah. And He could demonstrate both facts by healing the man. It was easier to *say* 'Your sins are forgiven' in the sense that no one could prove otherwise. It was harder to say 'Get up and walk', because there would be an immediate litmus test as to His power. *"'So that you may know that the Son of Man has authority on earth to forgive sins . . . '"* (or, 'In order that you may know I am the Messiah sent by God') . . . *He said to the paralysed man, "Get up, take your mat and go home."'*[12]

At once the man stood up, took what he had been lying on and started home. *'Everyone was amazed and gave praise to God. They were filled with awe and said, "We have seen remarkable things today."'*[13]

In other words, the penny began to drop. Jesus had effectively invited an investigation of His claim to Messiahship, had responded to that investigation by demonstrating His Messianic authority, and the people recognized the significance of what they had observed.

Another day they brought to Jesus a man who was possessed by an evil spirit that had caused him to be dumb and blind.[14] It is important to understand that, usually, blindness and dumbness were not caused by demon possession, but in this man that was the cause.

What we might miss, were we not aware of the list of Messianic miracles the rabbis had compiled, is that this was one such very significant miracle. Exorcism was not an uncommon practice. The typical procedure involved bringing the victim to a place of prayer, and asking the spirit to identify itself by name. You can see this demonstrated when Jesus asks that question and the spirit answers, *"'My name is Legion, . . . for we are many."'*[15]

But when a spirit has rendered its victim dumb, it is impossible to ascertain the name, and this generally made it impossible for the rabbis to cast out such a demon. Without a voice it was not possible for the spirit in the victim to identify itself. Without identification it was not possible to command it to come out. Hence they reasoned that if anyone was likely to have the power to exorcise a dumb spirit, it would be the Messiah. He would be able to cast out the demon because he would have knowledge of the name without having to ask for it. The record is very brief, simply saying, *'and Jesus healed him, so that he could both talk and see.'*[16]

The implication was immediately clear to those who witnessed that healing. *'All the people were astonished and said, "Could this be the Son of David?"'*[17]

'All the people', that is, except the Pharisees. They were obliged either to make the same conclusion or come up with some other explanation.[18] They chose the latter option, and declared that there was another way that Jesus could know the identity without asking, and that was if He was in some way in league with Beelzebub. They refused the opportunity to receive Jesus as Messiah.

Although from this date Jesus changed His ministry and tended to perform miracles on a different basis, and to present His teaching in a different format, there remained two other substantial occasions when He performed a Messianic miracle with the intention that they think again about His claims. Six months before He was crucified, while walking through the temple during the Feast of Tabernacles, His disciples asked Him why a blind beggar had been born blind.[19] Jesus refuted their suggestion that it might have been caused by his own sin and proceeded to heal the man.

The curing of an inherent affliction proved His claim. The Jews reasoned that a person was afflicted because he or one of his ancestors had sinned. To be able to cure an illness or disability that had been present from conception implied the ability to remedy the causal sin. When his neighbours saw the man healed, they realized this implication, and took the man along to the Pharisees, the primary issue being whoever had healed him must be Messiah.

The Pharisees were set hard in their prejudice by this stage, and refused to accept such a conclusion. *'"This man is not from God, for he does not keep the Sabbath."'*[20] Actually, Jesus had total respect for the Sabbath,[21] but little time for the fifteen hundred rules and regulations with which the rabbis had burdened the people in an effort to define precisely what one may or may not do during Sabbath hours. The people were confused by the reaction of the Pharisees, and questioned, *'"How can a sinner do such miraculous signs?"'*[22] Later the healed man was to say, *'"Nobody has ever heard of opening the eyes of a man born blind. If this man were not from God, he could do nothing.''* [23]

Just a few weeks later Jesus executed what was arguably His most significant Messiah miracle when He raised Lazarus from the tomb where he had been dead and buried four days. As a result, *'many of the Jews who had come to visit Mary and had seen what Jesus did, put their faith in him.'* [24] The expression 'Jews' in this context implies Jewish leaders. In response the Sanhedrin met and discussed the matter. They concluded, *''Here is this man performing many miraculous signs. If we let him go on like this, everyone will believe in him.'' * [25] So from that day on they plotted to take His life.

Many of the ordinary people believed in Him. Some of the leaders, such as Nicodemus, a member of the Sanhedrin, believed in Him. He had presented His credentials in a way with which Saatchi could never compete! Even Pilate was inclined to believe Him and announced: *''Here is the man!''* [26]

He came as Messiah and Redeemer of any who would accept Him as such and confess their trust in Him. John, an eyewitness of Jesus' remarkable ministry, claimed that even those 'signs' selected for use in his Gospel gave ample evidence that Jesus is verily the Messiah. *'These are written that you may believe that Jesus is the Christ, the Son of God, and that by believing you may have life in his name.'* [27]

It is vital that you consider for yourself Jesus' claims because ''' 'it shall be that everyone who calls on the name of the Lord will be saved.' '' ' ' ''In no one else is there salvation. His is the only name in all the world, given to mankind, by which you must be saved.'' [28]

[1]Daniel 9:25. [2]Dr D. Stern, Jewish New Testament Commentary, page 34. [3]John 20:30, 31. [4]John 7:31 (NIV, Barclay and Living Bible respectively). [5]John 7:48. [6]Matthew 11:3. [7]Matthew 11:4ff (Barclay). [8]See Luke 5:12ff (Barclay). [9]Luke 5:17. [10]Luke 5:20. [11]Luke 5:21. [12]Luke 5:24. [13]Luke 5:26. [14]Matthew 12:22. [15]Mark 5:9. [16]Matthew 12:22. [17]Matthew 12:23. [18]Matthew 12:24. [19]John 9:1ff. [20]John 9:16. [21]Mark 2:27ff. [22]John 9:16. [23]John 9:32. [24]John 11:45. [25]John 11:48. [26]John 19:5. [27]John 20:31. [28]Acts 2:21; 4:12 (Barclay).

There's no such colour as grey

YOU'RE WAKLING ROUND the supermarket with a friend. You pick up the milk and the bread, and head for the fruit and veg counter. As you select your tomatoes and apples, your friend takes a couple of grapes from a bunch and eats them. You're embarrassed in case you have been picked up on the video monitor, but you are also indignant that a friend has done something you feel is dishonest. So you tell him.

He flinches at the suggestion, and then begins to quote back at you occasions when your own honesty was 'up for question'. How about the time you were at the launderette and the coin-slot was jammed? Not only did you get your drying done free, but you pocketed the money that spilled out onto the floor too! What about last weekend when you were boasting about driving down the motorway from Manchester to London in under two hours? There was no way you could do that without breaking the speed limit.

If taking a couple of grapes is dishonest, then how do you justify taking advantage of a broken slot machine, or driving over the speed limit? Maybe your friend has a point.

Some issues in life are clear-cut. Others are grey. During our youth we tend to see things as very black or white, and get quite militant about them. Maturing makes us more inclined to realize there are lots of 'greys' which perhaps helps us to be more tolerant. Maturing as Christians produces both effects; we simultaneously see some moral issues more clearly defined and others as more difficult to decide upon. It all depends on the circumstances.

Frank was a young Christian who was saving for a stereo system with CD player, so that he could enjoy the inspiration of gospel music while he studied. The saving process was slow, and he was impatient. The trouble was that he wanted a decent system, not just a cheap one. But decent systems with a good brand name cost money. Since he was a student he didn't have that much in any given month to salt away in savings, and it seemed it could be another year or so before he could afford the kind of gear he wanted.

One afternoon his mate Chris said he had heard of someone selling a quality stacking system at a knock-down price. Apparently this guy had several good quality systems for sale, very cheaply, and you could almost name the brand you wanted. They went round to see them, and there was no disputing that the equipment was all up-market, at down-market prices. True, it was all second-hand, but it seemed to be in excellent condition. Frank was almost dribbling at the mouth by the time he had settled on one he favoured most, but he did not have the cash with him so he had to make arrangements to come back later.

As they walked away, Frank asked Chris whether he thought everything was above board. The vendor seemed like a decent man, but something made Frank uneasy. Chris was a bit more laid-back, and nothing seemed suspect to him at all. As far as he was concerned, people sold second-hand items all the time. Plenty of traders made a living buying and selling used merchandise. There was no crime in that. The fact that this vendor had such a variety of stock was not necessarily suspect. Besides which, Frank was an innocent customer, buying in good faith. He did not need to ask where they had come from because that was not his problem. It would be embarrassing to suggest they were illegal, only to find they were legitimate.

Frank salved his conscience by asking his parents for advice on the grounds that the sooner he could set himself up with the system he wanted, the sooner he could gain the inspiration of the gospel music. It would provide a positive alternative to all the 'junk' on radio and TV. But his parents did not give a very strong lead one way or the other. Effectively they said he was old enough to make his own decisions, and they left it to him to do what he thought best. He decided to go ahead and buy one.

To help him raise money to buy the CDs to play on his new system, Frank agreed to help a neighbour clear out the garage of the house where their old dad had recently died. In the process of sifting through the accumulated treasures of decades, Frank learned that the now empty house had just been burgled. While they were working, the police arrived and told them that there had been a long series of burglaries on that side of town in recent months, but that as yet they had no leads. The kind of property that was being stolen was always household commodities such as VCRs, TVs, stereos, cameras and so on, that could be sold on very quickly.

After the police had gone, the family asked Frank if he had any suggestions from his local knowledge as to who might be responsible. He didn't know how to respond. If he mentioned the supplier of his own stereo system — which, by the way, was positively *not* stolen from that household — he would feel terrible if he had pointed the finger at an innocent dealer. On the other hand, he might find himself on a charge for receiving stolen property if it turned out his supplier was 'bent'. He was inclined to think that Chris was right; 'What you don't know won't harm you.' The issue was not a clear-cut black and white issue, so he kept quiet.

A church administrator once went to buy a new word-processor for the church office, and asked for the price of the particular item that took his fancy. 'With or without a receipt?' the salesman asked. 'What difference does it make?' asked the churchman. *'About £150!'* came the answer. With a receipt, he would have to pay Value Added Tax. Without a receipt, it might be possible to be more creative! Should the churchman's priority be to get the best possible deal and save money for the church? Or should he pay over the odds to make sure he was 'rendering to Caesar that which was Caesar's'?

Imagine a scenario in which Ron is a young Christian and businessman, whose company has won a contract to construct a complete factory in a foreign country. Ron is obliged to travel to that country to arrange for building the premises and installing the plant. He is invited to take his wife Maggie with him on his first visit at company expense.

One of the members of their church has a mission for placing Bibles in foreign countries, especially in those where they are not readily available, and she sees an opportunity of persuading Ron and Maggie to take some in with them during their trip. She asks them to smuggle some in and deliver them to the address of the pastor of an underground church. They will need to be discreet at all times, and to keep

37

confidences because the liberty of Christian nationals may be at risk.

Before agreeing to the scheme, Ron and Maggie talk it over with some church friends. They realize that Bible smuggling is illegal in that country, otherwise there would be no need to smuggle them in. They know that they risk imprisonment. Maggie is inclined not to co-operate with the plan on the basis that she believes it wrong to violate civil law even in what seem extenuating circumstances, but will not make a fuss if Ron decides to go along with it. Some church friends argue that laws which restrict religious or civil liberties must sometimes be flouted in order to promote the work of the Gospel. Ron wonders what impact the discovery of smuggled Bibles might have on his company's contract, and where his highest loyalties must lie. He also realizes that the presence of Maggie on this one trip will provide the best possible cover for the scheme. Subsequent journeys alone may make him more vulnerable.

They decide to compromise by taking a smaller consignment which they would carry in a suitcase by air to a neighbouring country, and then conceal them among their luggage in a rented car to drive over the border. When they arrive at the border post, the guard asks specifically if they are carrying any religious material, particularly Bibles. Ron says, 'No!' They are admitted to the country, and breathe a sigh of relief that they were spared a thorough search of the vehicle. They even feel sure God had aided and abetted them.

When Ron and Maggie deliver the Bibles to their destination, the pastor invites them to a house meeting of the church that evening. They are reassured that so long as they maintain discretion, this will not pose a threat to local Christians or themselves. At the meeting the people are excited and grateful to have Bibles of their own for the first time.

Ron and Maggie feel the whole venture was worth the risk after all. Everything they had done was justified — except that one of the men at the meeting is the very border guard who looked Ron in the eye and asked him expressly whether he was smuggling Bibles. The guard seems agitated that Ron would lie so deliberately. Ron feels justified because he had no way of judging, under pressure, the disposition of the guard. He had no way of knowing the guard was actually a friendly Christian, and so had to presume hostility. The pastor intervenes with the suggestion that in some circumstances a Christian may be excused for behaving in an otherwise unacceptable way. It is called situation ethics. You apply ethical standards based upon what the situation may indicate, not upon any hard-and-fast predetermined code.

It is contorted enough, trying to sort out the 'wood' of our ethics from the proverbial trees, but it is distorted further by the human tendency to rationalize for convenience, personal conscience or comfort. We trivialize the Ten Commandments to suit ourselves. We salve our guilt by rationalizing that certain actions are justified or acceptable. We would even be inclined to argue with God about it.

I used to hate history class. All those dates to remember parrot-fashion. All those names and events to memorize. 'So what?' I thought to myself. 'Who cares?! What difference does it make? That was then; this is now!' Today I am a convert.

Perhaps this conversion is a sign of old age, but I prefer to think of it another way. The Apostle Paul believed that God inspired Scripture to be recorded with our good in mind. Scripture contains a lot of history, but it is there to help us because by reading it and contemplating what happened to others, we can learn something that may save our lives. For that reason, I love ferreting around in Old Testament stories, trying to come to grips with God's purpose in inspiring the record.

I put it to you that such scriptural rummaging is extremely beneficial. It is the source from which we establish our moral and ethical standards. It is the basis upon which we understand God. It acts as a mirror in which we can see our own defects and misconceptions reflected and, if we are humble and willing, recognize them for what they are. Allow me for a moment to suggest one possible lesson we may need to learn from ancient Babylon.

I have not been to Babylon. I have been to Jerusalem, and I have been to Damascus. I have been to Amman too, but

I have not been to Babylon. The closest I have got to visiting that ancient ruined city was in January 1977. Pastor Garth Anthony and I had the comfort of an air-conditioned bus ride from Damascus to the oasis city of Palmyra, which is perhaps halfway between Damascus and Babylon, across miles and miles of desert. There we were able to view what remains of a temple to the Babylonian god Bel and experience at least a little of a city influenced by Babylonian religious culture.

Ezekiel had no such comfort when he made the same journey back about 600 BC. Nor did he go voluntarily. He had not the remotest wish to taste Babylonian religion, nor any desire to visit Babylon at all. He despised everything to do with the Chaldeans. But King Nebuchadnezzar had other plans. He had invaded Judah and had defeated the Jews. As part of his method of dominating and subjugating uncooperative neighbouring states, he 'transplanted' all the aristocracy of a nation to another part of his empire where it would be impossible for them to motivate or lead any uprising against him.

Our interest in Babylon and Ezekiel is in a vision that he had concerning the spiritual condition of his people, because it also casts some light on our own predicament. In September 592 BC, we are told in Ezekiel 8, the elders of Judah had come to observe him outside his home and perhaps try to confer with Ezekiel what the message from God might be. Suddenly Ezekiel says, *'The hand of the Sovereign Lord came upon me'* and he was carried off in vision.[1] It felt as though he had been lifted by the hair of his head, and *'The Spirit . . . took me to Jerusalem.'*[2]

During this vision-trance, God took Ezekiel to four sites in Jerusalem, each time showing him another of the sins of the people, which they had rationalized away. It was not a pretty picture. The king had sponsored pagan worship by the introduction of a totem pole at the entrance of the temple. The elders, while pretending loyalty to God in public, secretly worshipped insects and creepy-crawlies. The women worshipped Tammuz. Some priests had turned their backs on God and His temple to worship the sun.

Perhaps the tragedy was that these people of influence had rationalized their behaviour and convinced themselves that it made no difference to their religious integrity. They felt secure in spite of their wayward standards. They gave the impression that God was ignorant of their lack of moral fibre. They said, *'''The Lord does not see us; the Lord has forsaken the land.''''*[3] God's response was, *'Tell them, Ezekiel, that their ways and thoughts are not hid from me, for I know what is going through their mind.'*[4]

Now if we take the Apostle Paul seriously, we will recognize that the various events in the history of Israel, tragic as they often were, were *'all warning markers — DANGER — in our history books, written down so that we don't repeat their mistakes,'* and that we are *'just as capable of messing it up as they were. Don't be naïve and self-confident. You're not exempt.'*[5] This means we need to look again at the Ezekiel vision and ask, 'In what ways did the people who got it wrong get it wrong, and in what ways did the people who got it right get it right?'

There are some obvious answers, and some perhaps less obvious ones. It is clear to us that if we accept the notion of the existence of God, then it is absurd to worship creepy-crawlies, mythological gods or goddesses, or a planet such as the sun or the moon. We cannot fudge such matters. These objects cannot possibly be or contain a Power capable of creating and sustaining the universe.

Because these issues are unequivocally black and white issues, we will not fall into the obvious mistake of worshipping totem poles, or stone or metal images. Nor, one hopes, will we fall into the error of denying God or turning our backs on Him. But will we fall into the less transparent mistake of assuming that God is not fully aware of our fudged excuses, our rationalized misdeeds and compromised shortcomings? The people of Judah comforted themselves with what was a basic inaccuracy, *'''The Lord does not see us!''''*[6]

Those people in Jerusalem who denied that they were in error had it wrong. Until they moved to a 'Chair No. 1' disposition and admitted the corrupt way they were, there could be no help and they condemned themselves. As God put it, *"'As for those whose hearts are devoted to their vile images and detestable idols, I will bring down on their own heads what they have done.'"*[7] God sees it all!

Yet God still loves us! Those people in the minority in Jerusalem who *"'grieved and lamented over all the detestable things that are done in it'"*,[8] got it right. To affirm and underpin their uncompromised humility, God promised He would fully transform their hearts and that is why He said, *"'I will give them an undivided heart and put a new spirit in them; I will remove from them their heart of stone and give them a heart of flesh. Then they will follow my decrees and be careful to keep my laws. They will be my people, and I will be their God.'"*[9]

Kind David made some serious mistakes when he lusted after Bathsheba, committed adultery with her, and had her husband Uriah placed in the front-line of battle to ensure his death. He convinced himself at the time of indulging his envy, that it was all right for a king to behave that way. But when Nathan confronted him with his sin, David did not deny it to God, and did not try to paper over it. What he had reasoned as being excusable or justifiable, he now frankly conceded was sin. He did not expect that God would merit him with credit points if he sorted the problems out himself. Instead he fell on God's mercy and depended upon Him to redeem the situation.[10] He asked God to create a new heart inside him that would not be subject to such vices, just as John Bunyan did, and in this way he 'got it right'. We must imitate David's response.

This is not to say we need flash our faults and errors around in public. God does not wish us to give any dimension of credibility to our sin or our sinfulness. It is only in our relationship with Him that we need totally disclose ourselves. When Jesus said, *"'Blessed are the poor in spirit, for theirs is the kingdom of heaven. Blessed are those who mourn, for they will be comforted'"*,[11] He was referring to the benefits of a recognition of our spiritual poverty and a mourning over our failures, but He had no time for those who did all such mourning in public view,[12] and insisted they will have received in full all the reward they are going to receive.

It is true that James advises *'Confess your sins to each other, and pray for each other, for that is the way to be cured.'*[13] However, this should not be understood to mean that if I have wronged Fred I need also to tell Jan, Dick and Mary. Not so. The person I need to sort it out with is Fred. I need to admit to him my error, apologize to him and ask his forgiveness. If I go on to tell Jan, Dick and Mary, there is a risk I will begin to glamorize my sin to some degree, and there should be no glamour in it, no basking in some kind of inverted pride.

We need to confess our sin but would be getting it wrong if we paraded our penitence in public, as we would be getting it wrong if we imitated those in Jesus' day whose *'"religion consists in ostentatious play-acting. . . . Their idea is to be seen praying by as many people as possible."'*[14]

Rather, knowing full well that 'God sees it all', even the most 'secret' sin, Jesus said, *'"Here's what I want you to do: Find a quiet, secluded place so you won't be tempted to role-play before God. Just be there as simply and honestly as you can manage. The focus will shift from you to God, and you will begin to sense his grace."'* Or as another translator put the same passage, *'"When you pray, go into your room, close the door and pray to your Father, who is unseen. Then your Father, who sees what is done in secret, will reward you . . . for your Father knows what you need before you ask him."'*[15]

When I was a youngster, one of our great treats was to have a holiday with our grandparents in Bournemouth. It had the benefits of being near to the sea, and near to the New Forest. It was nice to be spoilt, too!

I remember that when I was of junior school age, my dad took my two sisters and me to Bournemouth, and left us there for an extended holiday with Grandma and Grandpa. On one occasion when I was in their bathroom, supposedly brushing my teeth before bed, I noticed the way the paint had peeled above the basin, and with a little imagination I could see an animal shape. It just needed a little modification here and there to complete the picture. So I found a hair grip and used it to impress my masterpiece for all posterity. I somehow imagined that no one else would notice either the picture or the accumulation of paint and plaster that fell to the floor.

Over the period of our stay I added a number of other works of art to the walls of the bathroom and to the downstairs toilet, each time oblivious to the consequences of being caught. In due course, however, my deeds came home to roost. Grandma set a trap by checking her walls and floor after each of us children used the bathroom, and one day she confronted me with the evidence. I denied it, of course, because Grandma could be a very intimidating woman, and suddenly the prospect of the consequences made it uncomfortable to sit even before the implementation of punishment. This denial, I was to learn, only served to make the smacks more numerous and of greater intensity.

Afterwards, Grandma set me on her knee to talk about the situation. I got the usual speech about, 'This hurt me more than it hurt you', but I was not convinced until she told me she was much more upset that I would lie to her than that I had scratched the paintwork. Later I came to realize that God's responses to us are on the same level, and it hurts Him more that we deny or rationalize our shortcomings, than that we fall into temptation in the first place.

It takes a bit of bottle to open our lives to the scrutiny of God, and to let Him show us where our deficiencies lie. It seems easier to argue that so many issues in life are grey issues. Is it too much to suggest that with God there is no such colour as grey?

' "*Trivialize even the smallest item in God's Law and you will only have trivialized yourself. But take it seriously, show the way for others, and you will find honour in the kingdom.*" ' [16]

---

[1]Ezekiel 8:1. [2]Ezekiel 8:3. [3]Ezekiel 8:12. [4]See Ezekiel 11:5. [5]1 Corinthians 10:6, 11, 12 ('The Message' New Testament). [6]Ezekiel 8:12. [7]Ezekiel 11:21. [8]Ezekiel 9:4. [9]Ezekiel 11:19-20; Jeremiah 31:31-40; Deuteronomy 30:6. [10]Psalm 51. [11]Matthew

5:3, 4. [12]Matthew 6:5. [13]James 5:16 (Barclay). [14]Matthew 6:5 (Barclay). [15]Matthew 6:6-8 ('The Message' New Testament). [16]Matthew 5:19 ('The Message' New Testament).

Make every effort to be holy

'DADDY, CAN I have a kite?'

It was 1973. My family then consisted of Sheila, my wife, Nathan, our oldest son aged $4\frac{1}{2}$, and Bobby who was almost 2. We added Danny later. Sheila and I were with the boys at Oxwich, on the Gower Peninsula in South Wales, where I had been invited to serve as camp pastor at a summer camp for senior youth aged 16 to 25.

Two-string kites were all the rage that summer, and Nathan longed to have one of his own. On the other hand, I was not sure he could manage one just yet and, besides, they seemed rather expensive on the limitations of a minister's salary. But he kept on asking, 'Daddy, can I have a kite?' every day, several times a day. Every time, in fact, that he saw another kite flying.

Finally I gave in. Well, almost. I bought a single-string kite for 95 pence, which I thought was a bit more reasonable for a 4-year-old. Then I showed him how to fly it, by standing with his back to the wind, tugging gently on the string and letting the kite lift against the wind. He soon got the hang of it, and was reeling out more and more of the fifty metres of string. Not to worry, because the string was wrapped around a plastic handle at the end that should allow him to maintain control.

The lads from the camp had improvised a soccer pitch on the grass between the tents, and had a game in full swing. It was a deadly serious game in which those from the Balham and Brixton areas of London had assumed the names and roles of the Brazilian national team, and had taken on a 'Rest of the World' team.

Nathan stood a few feet from our tent where I was going over the devotional talk I was to present at the campfire that evening. The wind lifted his kite further and further over the soccer pitch, until he had spun out the whole length of the cord and it flew distant across the other side of the field.

When suddenly the football arrived at Nathan's feet, he politely reached down for it and threw it to one of the players, letting go of the kite string momentarily in the process. Unfortunately, the plastic handle had never been properly attached to the string, and he had let it drop, holding only the string-end. When he went to clasp the string again, naturally the wind had carried it away beyond his reach, and he wailed, 'Daddy my kite has gone!'

I was not about to see 95 pence fly away in the wind, so I sprang to my feet, scattering my notes everywhere as I did so, and ran straight through the middle of the soccer game chasing the end of the string, which was hovering tantalizingly six feet above the ground, but receding about as fast as I could pursue it. I had no time to explain or apologize; I just sprinted through the players, arm outstretched ready to retrieve the string if I caught up with it. The lads stood back in bewilderment, not sure what it was I was chasing, since they had no sight of either the kite or the string. As far as they were concerned, I was chasing thin air. Perhaps the camp pastor had finally lost his mind?

Across the other side of the soccer pitch, Pauline Sinclair was carrying a tray of drinks down to her husband Doug, our camp master, who was working at their caravan at the bottom of the field. She did not see me at first, but was startled when she did glimpse me approaching on collision course, hand still outstretched before me. She could not see the string or the kite either, but I had to continue my pursuit or lose the chase and, somehow, we avoided an impact.

At last I caught the string, and proudly began my return with it. I say 'proudly' but I was more than a little embarrassed, so I felt compelled to show the string first to Pauline and then to the soccer players so as to explain my odd behaviour. They still looked a little bemused, but at least I had retrieved the prized kite and had saved myself the expense of a replacement. It had been an effort. It had been rather embarrassing. No one else had understood what I was doing or why. But it was worth it, because if I had not made the effort the kite would have escaped me.

Whenever I read Hebrews 12:14, the experience of chasing Nathan's kite comes to mind: *'Make every effort to live in peace with all men and to be holy; without holiness no one will see the Lord.'* The older translations, such as the King

James Version, simply say, *'Follow peace with all men, and holiness.'* The Greek word means 'to run swiftly in order to catch some person or thing; to pursue, to seek after eagerly, earnestly endeavour to acquire'. It conveys the idea of pursuit of an objective in recognition that to fail to make the effort will mean that it will elude you. Hence, if you do not make the effort to attain holiness, it will elude you as surely as a kite borne on the wind will rise beyond your grasp.

There was a time when buses in England had the door at the rear corner, with an open platform and grab rails, which meant that it was possible to run after a bus if you had just missed it, and jump onto the platform. The picture that the phrase 'make every effort' should conjure up in your mind is that of someone chasing the bus and trying his best to get on to it, even though it has begun to move away from the stop, because if he did not make the effort it would leave without him. In the same sense, *'Make every effort to be holy'* because if you do not, it will elude you; you will fail to achieve the target God has set.

Pastor Ole Kendel tells the story of arriving by taxi cab at one of the major airports in the USA. His luggage and camera had been stowed in the boot (the 'trunk' if you are an American) by the driver. When they arrived at the terminal, before getting out of the cab, Ole paid the fare, then stepped out, expecting the driver to come to the boot and unload his luggage. Instead, to his surprise the driver sped off, leaving him stranded.

But Ole was not to be cheated that easily, and he realized that the route back to the road would take the cab round the car park to a junction controlled by traffic lights. Ole sprinted across the car park, leaping over car bonnets and boots on his way to reach his target in time. I am glad he made it, and the driver relinquished his property without much objection. Ole is normally a placid man, but I can well imagine he can be intimidating if riled! More importantly, if he had not made the effort, his luggage would have disappeared forever.

The New International Version uses the injunction *'make every effort'* in a handful of similar passages of exhortation.

'*Make every effort to be found spotless, blameless and at peace with God.*'[1]

'*Make every effort to add to your faith goodness; and to your goodness, knowledge; and to knowledge, self-control; and to self-control, perseverance; and to perseverance, godliness; and to godliness, brotherly kindness; and to brotherly kindness, love. For if you possess these qualities in increasing measure, they will keep you from being ineffective and unproductive in your knowledge of our Lord Jesus Christ.*'[2]

'*Make every effort to keep the unity of the Spirit through the bond of peace.*'[3]

'*Let us therefore make every effort to do what leads to peace and to mutual edification.*'[4]

'A-ha!' we will hear some exultant and relieved voices claim, 'There is human effort involved after all!' And then they will continue, 'Perhaps John Bunyan was not so wrong in working at reforming his behaviour. Perhaps he was right to seek a better standard of conduct and do his best to comply with God's requirements. This proves we *must* do our best to modify our real selves; so that we can move from the person we are, to becoming the person God wants us to be! We must do our best and then God will make up the difference. There *is* an expectation that we shall put the effort in, and there *is* merit in working our hardest to be good Christians!'

When Peter and Paul wrote these warnings, they were two of the most experienced and successful pastor-evangelists of the first century Christian Church. We will do well, therefore, to think carefully through what they have to say on the matter of holiness and the effort involved in achieving it. Our best move will be to reflect on their counsel under the following three headings:

1. Effort towards the objective of holiness *is* necessary;

2. This does *not* imply a change in the way God works for our salvation;

3. The changes called for involve fundamental root character qualities, not superficial cosmetic behavioural adjustments.

1. Effort towards the objective of holiness IS necessary!

The comment 'Without holiness no one will see the Lord,' is a fairly crucial comment to make and therefore absolutely critical to understand. It reflects the very words of Jesus, *"Blessed are the pure in heart, for <u>they</u> shall see God."* [5]

Peter also said something very similar when he wrote: *'Therefore, prepare your minds for action; be self-controlled; set your hope fully on the grace to be given you when Jesus Christ is revealed. As obedient children, do not conform to the evil desires you had when you lived in ignorance. But just as he who called you is holy, so be holy in all you do; for it is written, "Be holy, because I am holy."* [6]

God is very forthright in expressing His expectations of those who profess His name. Let it never be said that God is content to save us *in* our sins, or in other words that God will forgive us for our past and then turn a blind eye if we continue that way. His purpose is to save us *from* our sins, or in other words to forgive us for our past and then enable us to break free of it. When Jesus released the woman caught in adultery, He said to her, *"I don't condemn you . . . . Go and from now on stop sinning."* [7]

God is equally forthright in speaking to those 'believers' who cynically assume they can continue in sin and yet claim His acceptance and protection. To quote just one example, when God speaks through Jeremiah: *"Reform your ways and your actions, and I will let you live in this place. Do not trust in deceptive words and say, "This is the temple of the Lord, the temple of the Lord, the temple of the Lord!" . . . . Will you steal and murder, commit adultery and perjury, burn incense to Baal and follow other gods you have not known, and then come and stand before me in this house, which bears my Name, and say, "We are safe"* — safe to do all these detestable things?" [8]

If we were to put this into colloquial language, God would be saying: 'You people have a nerve! You live lives steeped in selfishness, and you seem to have little conscience or morality, much less any sense of the affront your paganism is to me, and then you come and stand here in worship with the assumption that you are safe because I would never let any mischief befall my city or my temple. That's not on!

Please radically change your ways and then we can really achieve things together, but as things are you are going to destroy yourselves.'

It is just as wrong today for a person who accepts Jesus as Messiah, and seeks forgiveness from God on that basis, to continue nonchalantly with a life indifferent to his or her shortcomings. Humans are always full of excuses intended to allow them to continue to indulge their sinful natures, but the Christian must overcome that tendency. The greatest handicap the Church has is the unsatisfactory lives of professing Christians. As Gandhi is quoted as saying, 'Christianity would be all very well were it not for the Christians!'

The test is not that one has heard the words of Jesus, nor even that one believes in them, but that one lives them, too. On that basis, Jesus told the parable of the wise and foolish builders: *'"Therefore everyone who hears these words of mine and puts them into practice is like a wise man who built his house on the rock."'* [9]

It is a simple thing to establish that the objective of holiness is mandatory; scripture after scripture can be cited to that end. The next thing we have to discuss is the question of what form that effort to achieve holiness must take, and how such radical changes may be achieved.

2. This does NOT imply a change in the way God works for our salvation.

We have established that the only basis upon which we may obtain reconciliation with God is that of approaching Him without pretence, admitting the way we are with all our faults and failures, in a private prayer which claims solely the merits of His Messiah, Jesus.

We have found that *'"Everyone who calls on the name of the Lord will be saved,"'* [10] that *'If we confess our sins, he is faithful and just and will forgive us our sins',* [11] and that *'"Then your Father, who sees what is done in secret, will reward you . . . for your Father knows what you need before you ask him."'* [12] It seems clear that no amount of solo effort on our part can successfully bridge the gap between our real selves and the expectations God has of us.

But with these 'make every effort' passages, we are

hearing suggestions that we must make the effort to pursue holiness, because without that effort holiness will elude us, and without holiness no one will see God. Indeed, it is much more than just a suggestion; it is a demand which is reinforced over and over in both Old and New Testaments. Can we resolve this apparent contradiction? Does this seem to imply, perhaps, that while our initial reconciliation with God must be on the basis of our humble confession that we are sinful and powerless to do anything about it, once we have been forgiven we have to pull out all the stops to achieve holiness, and that this must be achieved by basic human grit and commitment?

It will come as a relief to you to learn that this is a false picture, a false resolution of the dilemma. The basis upon which we grow in holiness is the same, exactly the same, as the basis upon which God receives us initially. God does not change His method of reconciliation half-way through the process. May I say again, consider often and with care, the following verses:

'To claim that we have no sin is an act of self-deception, and a proof that we have no idea of the truth. If we confess our sins, we can depend on him, even although he is just, to forgive us our sins, and to purify us from every kind of wickedness. To say that we have never committed a sin is as good as to call him a liar, and to prove that we have no idea what his message means.'[13]

The fantastic news of the Gospel is that not only is God willing to forgive us on the basis of our confession of sin and our profession of belief in Jesus, but God is also willing to take on our whole sin problem, so that on the identical basis of confession and profession, He will also undertake *'to purify us from every kind of wickedness!'*

The effort we have to make is not that of suppressing or subduing all our sins, but that of abandoning our conceit and arrogant independence, because the human heart is fundamentally flawed and incapable of victory on its own. As Paul acknowledged in his own struggle, *'When I want to do the right thing, the one thing that I can do is the wrong thing. In my inner self I delight in the law of God, but I am aware of a different law, operating in the physical parts of my body, and waging a constant campaign against the law which my reason accepts, and reducing me to captivity to that sinful principle which operates in my physical body. I am a wretched creature. Who will rescue me from this body which turns life into death? God alone can through Jesus Christ our Lord!'*[14] *'For it is God who is at work in you, to put into you the will to desire and the power to achieve what his purpose has planned for you.'*[15]

Paul felt that it was a tragedy when Christians could only see part of their way forward on the basis of their trust in God. He got 'uptight', as we say, when he heard that some religious teachers were implying that the basis of gaining holiness (called 'sanctification' by the theologians) was different from the basis of initial acceptance by God ('justification', as the theologians would say). He realized that he could not remain with every congregation that he had established in his evangelistic ministry, and that inevitably he would plant the seed and other ministers would water it. However, it dismayed him to hear that sometimes this watering was erroneous, especially if the false teaching encouraged reliance on works. He wrote to the converts at Corinth:

'By the grace God has given me, I laid a foundation as an expert builder, and someone else is building on it. But each one should be careful how he builds. For no one can lay any foundation other than the one already laid, which is Jesus Christ. If any man builds on this foundation using gold, silver, costly stones, wood, hay or straw, his work will be shown for what it is, because the Day will bring it to light.'[16] In other words, the building materials for growing more like the person God wants us to be are the same building materials as we started with — confession of our sin and total need of God's grace, and profession in Jesus as our Messiah. If anyone builds using other materials such as works, it will be exposed at the judgement.

Again he wrote to the Galatian Christians, *'Will you answer me one question? Did you receive the Spirit as a consequence of observing the law, or simply because you heard the offer and accepted the way of faith? How can you be so senseless? You began in the Spirit. Are you going to end up by trying to win salvation by doing something to your body? Are you simply going to write off all the great facts of your Christian experience? . . . Does he who gives you the Spirit so generously, and who works miracles among you, do so because you observe the law, or because you heard the offer and accepted the way of faith? You have exactly the same experience as Abraham. Abraham took God at his word, and that act of faith was accepted as putting him into a right relationship with God. So then, you are bound to see that it is the people who rely entirely on faith who are sons of Abraham.'*[17]

I hope it would not violate Paul's intention if we were to paraphrase this passage, and I would suggest the following: 'Let me ask you one question, When you sought peace with God, how did you approach Him? On the basis of your fine achievements or on the basis of humble trust in His promises? It was the latter! Well, then, do not "blow it" by reverting to your own cosmetic behavioural achievements, because to be a true son of God you must rely on Him from beginning to end.'

The reason for this is that the holiness that we are instructed to pursue earnestly is not something we can pull off ourselves because it has to do with fundamental root qualities, not just with superficial behavioural modifications.

3. The changes called for involve fundamental root character qualities, not superficial cosmetic behavioural adjustments.

You and I are like John Bunyan. If we decide that drinking, swearing, dancing, bell ringing or playing tipcat is unacceptable in the Christian, we can brace ourselves and modify our behaviour. Whatever list we care to develop, we can live up to if we give it enough effort. We can stop eating this, drinking that, saying certain words, going certain places, doing certain things on certain days.

The trouble is that while these matters may rightly be defeated as sins, in a sense they are merely symptoms of a fundamentally flawed nature which we have not begun to remedy. It is important to understand the difference between acts which are sins and a nature which is intrinsically sinful. We can trim up all the sins we might care to list, but there is little we can do to remedy our corruption at the core, which sooner or later will erupt and cause us to fall again.

William A. Miller tells a puzzling story of his childhood. He was raised by his uncle and aunt because his parents had died. One day a lady friend of the family, who was a frequent visitor to their home, called round at their back door. She was wearing a bright new summer dress that had a zip right down the front. As his uncle greeted her at the door, for some bewildering reason he took hold of the zip and undid it — completely.

'To this day,' wrote Miller, 'I wish I could have been able to capture the whole episode on film. There stood Mrs Davis with her dress hanging wide open, absolute astonishment etched into her face. My aunt stood two feet away in utter disbelief. And I in my childish innocence stood there giggling a little, but wondering too, if perhaps my uncle Lou had lost his mind.

'He soon regained his awareness and was feeling obvious shock and remorse. Very seriously he said, "My goodness, Helen, I'm sorry. I really am! I just don't know what came over me."

'Not until many years later did I realize that what "came over" my uncle that afternoon was . . . his "shadow"'.[18]

The 'shadow' to which Miller refers is the intrinsic sinful nature within the human heart. He remarks that in growing up we are trained to 'grow out of' or suppress undesirable tendencies of our nature such as aggression, lust, egocentricity. He continues:

'I am afraid, however, that this is the mistake we often make. . . . We think we have successfully got rid of these inferior, undesirable tendencies, when in fact all that happened is that they have been pushed into the background and stored away in the dark closets of our being, all the while continuing very much alive.'

The qualities that Peter listed are fundamental core character qualities, not merely superficial behaviour patterns. Faith, goodness, self-control, perseverance, godliness, brotherly kindness, love — are not easy to achieve in a consistent way. And because they are seated or unseated at the core of our character, the risk is that our sinful nature — 'shadow' — takes over and keeps bursting out, making it impossible for us to live a completely successful 'holy' life. By nature we do the rotten thing, not the good thing. Our attempts at radical change are futile because we are trying to work from the surface moving inwards.

God indicates He will accept responsibility for our whole sin problem *IF* we will make every effort to keep coming back to Him in submission. Precisely because it is a core 'heart' problem, He says, *'"I will remove from them their heart of stone and give them a heart of flesh. Then they will follow my decrees and be careful to keep my laws. They will be my people, and I will be their God."'* [19] With the changes that God brings, we find gradually we just do not want to do anything but His will. It would become an effort to do otherwise! God's work in us is inevitably going to succeed because it really is radical — He changes us from the core outwards.

'The Lord is the Spirit who gives them life, and where he is there is freedom from trying to be saved by keeping the laws of God. We Christians have no veil over our faces; we can be mirrors that brightly reflect the glory of the Lord. And as the Spirit of the Lord works within us, we become more and more like him.' [20]

Let me repeat it again in order that it may be beyond confusion. The Bible does demand that human effort is involved in achieving holiness, *BUT* we must not confuse what this effort is for, nor what it accomplishes in and of itself. We can neither obtain initial forgiveness (justification) nor fulfil holiness (sanctification) by even the most ardent solo human effort. If we expend our energy seeking salvation on that basis, we fool ourselves. Our relentless effort must be towards conceding to God our sin and our inability to do *anything* to remedy it — except keep coming back to Him in surrender.

Earlier chapters have suggested the futility of trying to achieve peace with God and respectability in His eyes by means of solo human determination and behaviour reform for 'Brownie points'. Subsequent chapters will address a number of things that self-disciplined effort can affect positively. Meanwhile be reassured by the noble declaration of St Paul: *'I can do everything through him who gives me strength.'*[21]

---

[1]2 Peter 3:14. [2]2 Peter 1:5-8. [3]Ephesians 4:3. [4]Romans 14:19. [5]Matthew 5:8. [6]1 Peter 1:13ff. [7]John 8:11 (Barclay). [8]Jeremiah 7:1-11. [9]Matthew 7:24. [10]Acts 2:21. [11]1 John 1:9. [12]Matthew 6:6-8. [13]1 John 1:8-10 (Barclay). [14]Romans 7:21-23 (Barclay). [15]Philippians 2:13 (Barclay). [16]1 Corinthians 3:10ff. [17]Galatians 3:2ff (Barclay). [18]W. A. Miller, *Why Do Christians Break Down?*, page 44. [19]Ezekiel 11:19ff. [20]2 Corinthians 3:17-18 (Living Bible). [21]Philippians 4:13.

The chicken syndrome is *not* for you!

AGRI OF AFRICA was to his people in Ghana akin to what Gandhi had been to the people of India. Like Jesus, Agri sometimes taught in parables. What follows is a customized version of an Agri parable I first heard on the radio, which I hope does him justice:

Kofi lived in Africa. Like most people, he used some land just beyond the village on which to grow vegetables and corn for his family. He also had a few cattle to provide milk and meat. And he had some hens which became such a fascination that he became obsessed by the variety of chicken breeds that existed. If he had opportunity to pass through other villages, he would look to see if anyone had types that he did not have, with the intention that he would acquire some for his collection.

In time he began to gather other kinds of birds, too. At first it was ducks and geese but then he became more adventurous and added guinea-fowl, pheasants, partridges, peahens and peacocks, indeed, any kind of fowl that he could find that might blend into his collection. One day when near to mountains several miles from his home village, he came across a baby eagle that had somehow fallen to the ground and been abandoned injured. Kofi decided he would take it home and attempt to raise it. He nursed the baby eagle with his other birds, and soon it began to recover and to peck around on the ground, imitating the hens with which it lived. Even after it was completely healed and had grown very large, it stayed with them and pecked at the grains and grit just as they did.

One day a stranger came through the village, and Kofi invited him home for something to eat and somewhere to stay. They sat that evening conversing and watching the sunset as Kofi's wife prepared the meal. As they spoke, Kofi's collection of fowl came into view, pecking at the ground looking for food. When the stranger saw the eagle, which by now was an impressive full-grown bird, he was startled to see a bird of prey with the hens and blurted out, 'You have an eagle in with your hens!'

'Yes, I know,' said Kofi, 'but it's all right because I have had him since he was small and he is happy with my hens and never attacks them. In fact, he seems to think he is a chicken and he lives very contentedly with them.'

'I can't believe it!' the stranger said, and for the rest of the meal he could hardly take his eyes off the bird, repeatedly musing to Kofi, 'I've never seen anything like this!'

The meal over and his appetite satisfied, the stranger was still troubled by this strange phenomenon and said to his host, 'I am sure that bird would rather fly off and choose to live as an eagle, if you would just give it a chance.'

'I have given it a chance,' Kofi reassured him. 'You can see for yourself he is not tied down or fenced in. He can take off anytime, but he is happy thinking he is a chicken, and I am happy that he stays with us.' But to allay any further curiosity, Kofi agreed that the stranger could experiment with his theory. The two men walked over to the birds, Kofi put out his hand and the eagle hopped up onto it and was lifted as high as Kofi could reach. The stranger then tried to persuade the eagle, 'Eagle, you are an eagle not a chicken. You belong to the sky and not to the ground. Stretch out your wings and fly!'

The eagle just looked at him, then looked at Kofi, then looked at all the hens, and jumped back down onto the ground and started picking at the grains again. 'There you are,' said Kofi. 'I told you he is happy just to be a chicken.'

'I still can't believe it,' said the stranger. 'Will you let me try something else first thing tomorrow morning?' So, long before the sun rose, Kofi and the stranger took the eagle and walked out through the forest to the foothills of the mountains where Kofi had first found him. As the sun rose, Kofi held the eagle up high again, and the stranger gave the same speech, this time holding the bird so that he could catch the glint of the sun rising over the mountain tops.

'Eagle,' he said, 'you are an eagle, not a chicken! You belong to the skies and not to the earth. Stretch out your wings and fly!' This time, with the sun in his eyes and the wind teasing his magnificent plumage, the eagle stretched out its wings and began to fly, further and further towards the sun over the mountains. It never returned. It was an eagle! And it was free!

We do not need to labour the parable at all. The meaning should be fairly clear. For too long the enemy of mankind has deluded and distracted us with the message that all we have is here and now, that we are chickens with no purpose but to pick around on this earth for a living, and no destiny but the grave. Satan has pulled the wool over human eyes to such an extent that even those who *do* realize that there is a better way and a nobler purpose for mankind find themselves defeated in trying to attain to it. *'The god of this world has blinded the minds of those who refuse to believe, with the result that they cannot see the light that has dawned on them, the light of the good news of the glory of Christ, who is exactly like God.'*[1]

'Satan is seeking to veil Christ from our sight, to eclipse His light; for when we get even a glimpse of His glory, we are attracted to Him.'[2]

'''It is no use!'''' the Judaeans claimed. *'''I love foreign gods, and I must go after them.''''*[3] They felt locked inescapably into their life-style. They were defeated and demoralized. 'What's the point of trying?' they were saying in effect, 'because the harder we try, the worse we seem to become ensnared! We may as well remain chickens!'

But the chicken syndrome is not for us! *'Those who hope in the Lord will renew their strength. They will soar on wings like eagles; they will run and not grow weary, they will walk and not be faint.'*[4] This is possible because of the sure word of God, *'''Return . . . ; I will cure you of backsliding.''''*[5]

When I left school and joined the Norfolk Constabulary as a police cadet back in 1961, one of my noble tasks was to make the morning tea and coffee for all the policemen in the station. Towards the rear of the station we had a room that served a number of purposes. It was the Parade Room in which the whole Division assembled for a pep-talk from the Superintendent on pay days. It was also the Charge Room where specific criminal charges were formally presented to those in custody. But its most popular use was as the tea room. At about 11am each day I would ring round the station to tell them all it was ready.

I can still recall clearly one such morning. The Duty Sergeant and the Detective Inspector (the 'DI') were talking with the policewoman and a patrol car driver, huddled around the charge desk. Scattered round the room in similar huddles were about fifteen other officers of various ranks. As I passed by the group at the desk, I could hear that they were discussing the existence of God. I knew the DI was a firm Methodist, that Sergeant Howes was a Christian man but one who rarely attended church, and that WPC Wells was the kind of Christian who went to church only at Christmas or Easter. The patrol driver was a hard-nosed secular man who felt he had witnessed too much misery at road accidents to sustain belief in God.

As I passed the group a second time, the DI called out to me, 'Cadet, do you believe in God?' That moment the whole Parade Room went quiet as every officer turned to hear my response. The usual loud conversation fell to total silence. You could hear the proverbial pin drop. I did believe in God. The DI had seen me at an evangelistic meeting and was calling on me for support to show that some young people did believe in God. But I was overwhelmed by the assumed hostility of the rest of the officers. I interpreted their silence to indicate scorn, and felt too intimidated to speak up positively, so I said, 'No.'

The DI was not about to be deflected, so he gave me another chance, speaking as if perhaps I had not heard the question clearly the first time. But having said 'No' once, it was even more embarrassing to change my tune than it would have been to say 'Yes' the first time. So I repeated, 'No!'

I suppose I can shelter under the claim of good company, because in vaguely similar circumstances Peter had denied Jesus long before I had. He did it three times! He even swore and cussed at the very suggestion. But I cannot find solace in hiding behind such an excuse. To this day I wished it had been on video tape so that I could go back and re-record my response, this time asserting in a clear voice, 'YES!' It is too late for that, as it is too late for the many subsequent times my mouth or my life has denied Him. I could give up and say, 'It's no use! I am too weak. I am a born coward, and I do not deserve Christ's standing up for me. He did say that those who deny Him, He would deny.' To do so would be like hopping down from Kofi's hand and resuming life as a chicken. That's not for me. I will keep on going, and I will learn more and more to relinquish my weaknesses to the Holy Spirit so that He may remedy them.

There was an occasion when the remnant of Jews who remained in Jerusalem asked Jeremiah to pray for guidance on their behalf. They wanted to know that they were doing God's will, so they asked the prophet to pray, with the promise that whatever the answer, whether it was a comfortable answer or an uncomfortable one, they would commit themselves to doing what God indicated. It all seemed so genuine and brave, but it turned out to be phoney. They would only do what God indicated *if* it coincided with what they already planned. You can read about it in Jeremiah 42.

If that had been a one-off situation, they could have received God's correction and bounced back, but it was a persistent fault. They had repeatedly claimed freedom. *'"We are free to roam"'* had been the cry of God's people for many a year. *'"He will do nothing! No harm will come to us; we will never see sword or famine."'* In their indignant claim to freedom of action they continued to maintain the chicken syndrome, and conformed to the pattern with which Satan had distracted their minds.

'Do not conform any longer to the pattern of this world, but be transformed by the renewing of your mind' Paul wrote to the Christians in Rome.[7] *'Don't let the world around you squeeze you into its mould, but let God re-make you so that your whole attitude of mind is changed'* is the way J. B. Phillips so aptly translated the same verse. Placed into Agri's parable, that verse could read, 'Do not be hoodwinked into settling for the chicken mentality, but be converted by allowing God to lift your vision.'

Such conversion, transformation, or renewing calls for a fundamental change in our values, motivation, and objectives. In order to change these, we must know what God's values and objectives for us are. We must know the truth about sin, and we must know the truth about righteousness, because it is *'the knowledge of truth that leads to godliness'.*[8] We will continue to love picking around in the grain and grit like chickens until we learn how despicable that is. We will persist in being transfixed by Satan's delusion until we see clearly how contemptible it is to God and how destructive it is to us. To gain such an awareness of truth, we must diligently study the Word of God.

'Yawn, yawn!' I hear you cry. 'Boring!'

Well, perhaps that is because you have done it the hard way up till now. There is no reason to labour through from Genesis to Revelation, because invariably you will give up with all the 'begets'. Instead, find yourself a dynamic modern translation and read the Gospels over and over, big chunks at a time if you can. Get a feel for the person that Jesus is, and the values He holds dear. Then read through Acts and get a feel for the power of the Holy Spirit in action in the early Church. Then you could try something ambitious such as reading Jeremiah through from one end to the other, not at a single sitting but over a period of days. This will give you a feel for the purity of God, the high standard of His expectations, the folly of humankind, and the desperation of settling for the chicken syndrome. In time you will find the Bible hard to put down, not boring at all!

The work of transforming our minds is the work of the Holy Spirit, who is given as a gift from God, but providing access for the Holy Spirit to our minds is a matter of personal discipline. The combined process is what Jerry Bridges has called 'dependent discipline'.[9] He continues, 'The word *discipline* sums up our responsibility to grow in holiness. The qualifying word *dependent* emphasizes our need for God's work in all we do.' Spending time in Bible reading simply allows the Holy Spirit to access your mind in order that He may renew it. But if you prefer to remain a chicken brain, stay with the TV!

'We have a clever enemy who subtly convinces us that it is better to discuss our problems than to treat them decisively with the strong antibiotic of God's Word. How then do we find solutions from the Word for everyday living and for special problems as they come along? One of the ways God uses most often with me is to bring to my mind a portion of Scripture I have memorized. It's exciting to see how in a moment of personal need or in counselling or encouraging someone else, I find the Holy Spirit brings to my mind a verse which fits perfectly, one I may not have thought of for a long time. So I am personally sold on memorizing Scripture as a regular process of "stocking the pantry", storing God's words of wisdom in my mind and heart.'[10]

As the transformation of your mind gets under way, you will find yourself confronted with more and more occasions when you must choose. Some choices can be made deliberately and with reflection; others must be made spontaneously and instantly, becoming a new second nature to us. You hit your thumb with the hammer, and you choose not to swear. A colleague causes you to trip over a bag; you choose not to make an issue of it. A magazine confronts you with pornographic pictures; you choose to pass them over. You have opportunity to delay your own schedule to help someone else with his; you choose to do so without a second thought. Peter talks of those who *'train themselves to be greedy; and are doomed and cursed.'*[11] That is conforming to the world's pattern. You now choose to 'train yourself' to be generous. That is God's pattern. And that is 'dependent discipline'. How else can you hope to be a 'disciple'?

Do not be alarmed if during this dependent discipline you seem to be going backwards, because the more you learn of God's holiness the more you realize how great the gulf is between yourself and Him. Do not be alarmed at the discovery and do not be alarmed at the seemingly impossible bridging of the gulf. Learn from the helpful self-analysis that Paul records during his journey to holiness. Notice the way his self-perception is re-evaluated and toned down in course of time, as follows.

In AD48, early in his writing ministry, Paul proudly laid claim to the highest calling, writing to the Galatians: *'Paul, an apostle — sent not from men nor by man, but by Jesus*

Christ and God the Father.'[12] Seven years later he had experienced some mellowing, some 'renewing' of his mind, when he wrote to the Corinthians: *'For I am least of the apostles and do not even deserve to be called an apostle.'*[13] A further eight years of the influence of the Holy Spirit and Paul assessed himself *'less than the least of all God's people'.*[14] Even that evaluation was surpassed a little later when he wrote to Timothy, *'Christ Jesus came into the world to save sinners — of whom I am the worst.'*[15] Such a progression is neither accidental nor coincidental, for as the Holy Spirit is allowed increasing access to the human mind, so our perspective becomes more and more realistic.

Nor should such a progression become daunting. It is not that we are losing the battle or becoming more and more sinful, but that we are more clearly aware of the extent of the sinfulness that has always been present. If as a result we allow our feelings to become depressed at lack of progress, we have missed the point. The closer we come to Jesus, the more apparent our deficiencies will appear, but that should make us feel reassured, not overwhelmed.

The remaining vital companion to allowing the Spirit access to our minds for renewal, and to making choices for positive change in our lives, is the practice of prayer. We need to ask God to help us to understand truth. We need to ask Him to make us alert to sinful desires which well up from inside ourselves or which invade us from outside ourselves. We need to pray that God will reveal to us ways in which we are failing to live according to the truth.

We need to pray for strength to make the right choices; for persistence in allowing the Spirit access to our minds via Bible reading. We must have daily, tenacious, persevering prayer, asking God to enable us in our discipline, and we should add to that the habit of brief, spontaneous prayers during the heat of battle of the day — moments when we simply call out, 'Lord, help me!'

Breaking away from the chicken syndrome can be paralleled with the work of a horticulturist. Imagine Alan Titchmarsh (of TV gardening fame) sitting in a greenhouse with a packet of tomato seeds, willing them to grow and produce an abundant crop. He can 'will' until the proverbial cows come home, but it will do no good because he is not completing those aspects of the task of which he is capable. He can prepare the soil, plant the seeds, provide irrigation, light and nutrition, but he cannot physically make anything grow. God undertakes the supernatural task of triggering the seed to growth and developing the seedling to maturity. Titchmarsh can then assist by protecting that growth by providing canes to resist the wind or withstand the weight of the developing fruit.

In the same way, you and I are wasting our time trying to be holy by will power. But there are tasks of which we are capable, and upon which the process of growth is dependent. We can prepare the soil by providing access to our minds for the Holy Spirit. We can irrigate and fertilize the germinating seed by spending time in the Scriptures. We can enable strengthening, positive choices to be made by staking up the new plant with canes of prayer. If ever we falter, as we surely will, there is no cause to give up in dismay. As John put it, *'If anybody does sin, we have one who speaks to the Father in our defence — Jesus Christ, the Righteous One.'*[16]

'Therefore, since we have a great high priest who has gone through the heavens, Jesus the Son of God, let us hold firmly to the faith we profess. . . . Let us then approach the throne of grace with confidence, so that we may receive mercy and find grace to help us in our time of need.'[17] Then we shall break away from conformity to this world, and shall be found among the *'mature, who by constant use have trained themselves to distinguish good from evil'.*[18]

'I went down to the potter's house, and I saw him working at the wheel. But the pot he was shaping from the clay was marred in his hands; so the potter formed it into another pot, shaping it as seemed best to him. Then the word of the Lord came to me: "O house of Israel, can I not do with you as this potter does?"'[19] That prophecy was made as a threat because of Israel's stubbornness, and God predicted, *'"They will reply, 'It's no use. We will continue with our own plans; each of us will follow the stubbornness of his evil heart.'"'*[20]

The choice is yours, but the chicken syndrome is certainly not for me!

---

[1]2 Corinthians 4:4 (Barclay). [2]*SDA Bible Commentary*, vol. 6, page 1097. [3]Jeremiah 2:25. [4]Isaiah 40:31. [5]Jeremiah 3:22. [6]Jeremiah 2:31; 5:12. [7]Romans 12:2. [8]Titus 1:1. [9]Jerry Bridges, *The Pursuit of Holiness*, NavPress 1978. [10]Betty Skinner, *Discipleship Journal*, Issue 20. [11]2 Peter 2:14 (Living Bible). [12]Galatians 1:1. [13]1 Corinthians 15:9. [14]Ephesians 3:8. [15]1 Timothy 1:15. [16]1 John 2:1. [17]Hebrews 4:14, 16. [18]Hebrews 5:14. [19]Jeremiah 18:3-6. [20]Jeremiah 18:12.

Gaius was a 'goodie', but how?

GAIUS WAS A common name in the first century, as common as 'John' is to us. It was a working class name, and there is evidence of a number of men with that name in the New Testament. There was a Gaius in Corinth, baptized by Paul, and another mentioned in Romans 16. There was a Gaius caught up with Paul in a riot in Ephesus, and possibly another who came from Derbe who also travelled with Paul. But the one we are interested in was a convert of John.

Very few personal letters have been preserved in the New Testament. Letters to Timothy and Titus are obvious exceptions, but those men were fellow-evangelists of Paul, younger men who needed specific instruction that he sent as personal letters which have survived as part of Scripture. Philemon was a Christian convert who qualified for a personal letter because of the unique circumstances of his former slave Onesimus; so Paul wrote directly to him and that letter has endured as Scripture. 'The chosen lady and her children', to whom John wrote his second letter, may have been individuals but the phrase is more likely to be 'code', a figurative designation of a local church. Then there was Gaius. He was the recipient of John's third letter.

You can read the whole letter in less than two minutes, because when John wrote it he used only one sheet of paper, expecting to be able to visit Gaius in person shortly afterwards. Within it we find reference to four men: 'The elder', commonly accepted to be John the beloved disciple and apostle; Gaius whom we might classify as a 'goodie'; Diotrephes, whom we might be inclined to classify as a 'baddie'; and Demetrius, another of John's associates who acts as postman to deliver the letter.

Gaius is commended by John because he is evidently *'walking in the truth'*. Perhaps we may take it from John's prayer that Gaius *'may enjoy good health'* that he was not too well physically. He was doing well spiritually, however, and John just wished that his physical health was as good. Indeed, reports of Gaius' religious consistency lifted John no end, so he encouraged Gaius by letter; *'I have no greater joy than to hear that my children are walking in the truth.'*

We should not conclude from that remark that Gaius was John's son. Often an evangelist looks upon those he has won to Christ as his 'children', and it is true that little gives as much pleasure to a pastor than to hear, after his ministry has called him on to other fields of labour, that those converts he left behind have remained faithful. Gaius probably was one of many men and women whom John's ministry had introduced to Christ, and it is because of that bond that John is so delighted with reports that have reached him via some itinerant preachers who had passed by Gaius' home and even found lodging and hospitality there.

That we may understand what John meant by the expression 'walking in the truth', we should compare and contrast it with similar phrases in his other letters. In his second, the one addressed to 'the chosen lady and her children', John refers to *'Many deceivers, who do not acknowledge Jesus Christ as coming in the flesh,'*[1] pointing out that these self-appointed ministers have *'gone out into the world'* on their own itinerant evangelistic mission. You may wonder why anyone who did not acknowledge Jesus would wish to venture out evangelizing; so it will be worth while digressing in order to explain.

By definition, converts to Jesus came from either a Jewish background or a Gentile background. Each had his own problem in fully accepting that Jesus was the Messiah who had come in the flesh. The Jew knew that Jesus of Nazareth was a human being, so had no problem with the 'coming in the flesh' part, but he often struggled with the question of His divinity. The Gentile often had the opposite problem because the influence of his Greek religious background taught him that God and goodness were spirit, while evil and badness were material — flesh and blood. For him the difficulty was in accepting that God could contaminate Himself by actually becoming real flesh. So he resolved his dilemma by teaching that Jesus just 'appeared' to be flesh but remained spirit. Greeks who held those beliefs were known as 'docetics', and there were many of them in the early Church, Cerinthus being a prime example.

Whichever 'camp' you came from, if you could not with full conviction confess that Jesus of Nazareth is the Messiah come in the flesh, then you had an inappropriate and inaccurate comprehension of Jesus' incarnation. *'Any such person'*, John says, *'is the deceiver and the antichrist. Anyone who runs ahead and does not continue in the teaching of Christ does not have God.'*[2] Clearly 'running ahead' is not the same as 'walking in' the truth.

In his first letter, John states: *'God is light; in him there is no darkness at all.'* Hence, *'If we claim to have fellowship with him yet walk in the darkness, we lie and do not live by the truth.'*[3] Evidently in John's thinking, 'walking in the darkness' implies a lagging behind, a reluctance to move along with Christ, and a reticence to allow Christ to make the changes in our lives that would result in 'walking in the light', *'but if we walk in the light, as he is in the light, we have fellowship with one another, and the blood of Jesus, his Son, purifies us from all sin'.* We may therefore conclude that to 'walk in the darkness' is not the same as 'walking in the truth'.

We used to have a family pet, a Springer Spaniel we called 'Barney'. Sometimes I think we should have named him 'Barmey', he was so senseless. He understood our commands, and, for example, would go to his bed when we called 'Bed!' to him; but as soon as his feet touched the bed he seemed to assume that he had fulfilled his part of the bargain, and he promptly came off it again. When we walked him, he never could bring himself to walk at heel. We tried all the techniques, including using a choke-chain in place of a usual collar and lead, but he was incorrigible.

Perhaps this was because by breeding he should never have been expected to walk to heel. Springer Spaniels are, after all, bred to be gun dogs, chasing wildfowl and rabbits for their masters. Consequently, Barney hated being limited to walking beside us — he wanted to run ahead and do what came in his genes.

Whippendell Wood was not far from our home, and it

was a favourite place to which I would take Barney when I wanted to walk and think. Taking him there killed two birds with one stone, so to speak, because it exercised both of us and gave me opportunity to think things over that I may have been wrestling with.

On one such occasion I had been reading John's letter to Gaius and had been contemplating what John meant precisely by the phrase 'walking in the truth'. True to form, Barney took off in front of me as soon as I released him from his lead. We walked for miles, and the whole time he was surging ahead of me, trying to anticipate my route each time we came to a junction, and all the time sniffing out birds and rabbits, squirrels and anything else that moved. Finally we came back almost to the car park, and came across a lady out walking her dog, but she had the opposite problem from mine. Her dog just was not interested in walking at all. It was clear he wanted to get back in the car and go back home to stretch out near the hearth. He was over-weight and ageing, and she had to wait for him every few strides because he had no desire to keep pace with her.

It was as if God had used the two dogs to help me understand what John was thinking of when he commended Gaius. 'Walking in the truth' is like 'walking with the Master', not running ahead out of control, wilful and doing your own thing; not loitering behind, showing reluctance even to associate with the Master, but walking stride-by-stride with Him. Or as Paul put it, *'If the Spirit is the ruling principle of our lives, we must march in step with the Spirit.'*[4]

So we may conclude that Gaius had accepted the Gospel and was responding to its standards. This is evidenced by the specific actions for which he is commended. He was told he was *'faithful in what you are doing for the brothers'*; he was putting his love for the truth into action; he was showing *'hospitality to such men so that we may work together for the truth'.* Those early days of the church were epitomized by itinerant preachers who gave up everything *'for the sake of the Name'* and *'went out, receiving no help from the pagans'.* Christians could receive them and provide hospitality to help in their missionary work, or they could decline such help and impede the work. Gaius was lending support, not for brownie points so that he could receive human acclaim or divine approval, but because he was already so devoted to the Lord he was walking in the truth.

In contrast, Diotrephes *'loves to be first', 'gossips maliciously about'* the church leaders, *'refuses to welcome'* those wandering evangelists, and even *'stops those who want to do so and puts them out of the church'.* Also in contrast, Diotrephes is an aristocratic name, not a popular name used among the working class. It was as rare as Gaius was common. So perhaps because of his high social status, Diotrephes was having trouble coming to terms with a subordinate role in his local church, and was clamouring for the leadership, imposing himself into that post. He was not quite 'in step with the Spirit', but at least he was in the church, and we must return to examine his case later.

Meanwhile, we must ask ourselves, 'What made the difference for Gaius?' Gaius was a 'goodie', but *how?* We will find the answer by returning to the promise God made to His people, even while they were still in captivity to the Babylonians, and by demonstrating how that promise was fulfilled to Gaius.

God's promise reads, *' " 'I will sprinkle clean water on you, and you will be clean; I will cleanse you from all your impurities and from all your idols. I will give you a new heart and put a new spirit in you; I will remove from you your heart of stone and give you a heart of flesh. And I will put my Spirit in you and move you to follow my decrees and be careful to keep my laws. . . . I will save you from all your uncleanness.' " '*⁶

Sprinkling with water was a ritual familiar to the Jewish people since Moses' day. Aaron and the priests were to sprinkle themselves each time they entered the sanctuary;⁷ houses that had been declared clean after a suspected case of house plague were to be sprinkled;⁸ people who had been in contact with a corpse, and their tent-homes, were to be sprinkled;⁹ and Zechariah had been told in vision that with the coming of Messiah, *' "a fountain will be opened to the house of David and the inhabitants of Jerusalem, to cleanse them from sin and impurity."'*[10] John the Baptist was able to make use of that association with spiritual cleansing, by inviting people to repent, and *'they were baptized by him in the Jordan River.'*[11] Gaius would have been immersed in baptism when he accepted Jesus as Messiah.

The illustration may be tired from over-use, but it is still the case that if you place a ball of soft clay alongside a ball of wax in the direct sunlight, the one will grow less and less impressionable and more resistant to change, while the other will become more and more sensitive and susceptible. Humanity displays the same characteristic when placed in the direct path of God's light and warmth. Pharaoh became more and more stubbornly opposed to God as God tried to melt his resistance;[12] Gaius' heart melted and as a result he demonstrated love in his life and 'walked in the truth'.

Because *'the heart is deceitful above all things and incurably sick',*[13] God promised a spiritual heart-transplant by which He would transform the impregnable into something pliable and teachable. He achieves this by the ministry of the Holy Spirit whom, God says, *'"I will put in you"'.*[14] He is a free gift! This presence of the Spirit transforms humans beyond recognition, enabling them to *'follow my decrees and be careful to keep my laws'. 'I tell you,'* said Jesus, *'and it is true, that unless a man is born again from above, he can have no experience of the Kingdom of God. . . . Unless a man is born of water and the Spirit, he cannot become a member of the Kingdom of God.'*[15] Gaius had been 'born again'.

The promise of the Holy Spirit in the life of the believer was linked inseparably with turning his back on Babylon. In Ezekiel's context it had to do with physically migrating from Babylonia back to the land God had promised. In Gaius and in all those who accept God's way of salvation, it has a spiritual application and is linked with abandoning the Babylonian ethic, so captivating to our psyche; abandoning all attempts to be saved by merit.

Gaius was a 'goodie'; in other words he lived and exhibited a victorious Christian life, because of the activity of the Holy Spirit in his life. This implies that Gaius consistently approached God in a 'Chair No. One' mentality, admitting to Him the way he was and that without God he could never fundamentally change.

The very confession that Jesus is the Christ is proof that the Holy Spirit was at work in his heart. When Peter responded to Jesus by saying *'"You are the Christ, the Son of the living God"'*[16], Jesus commended him, *'"This was not revealed to you by man, but by my Father in heaven."'* When Nicodemus came to Jesus to ask Him if He was Messiah, Jesus informed him he would never be able to grasp that fact until he had been *'"born again . . . born of the Spirit."'*[17] Paul affirmed that *'no one can say, "Jesus is Lord" except by the Holy Spirit.'*[18] Gaius had been 'born of the Spirit'.

Consequently, Gaius had benefited from radical spiritual heart surgery, the natural results of which are known as the fruits of the Spirit, namely: *'love, joy, peace, patience, kindness, goodness, faithfulness, gentleness and self-control,'*[19] virtually the same list as Peter recommended the believer *'make every effort'* to achieve — *'faith . . . goodness . . . knowledge . . . self-control . . . perseverance . . . godliness . . . brotherly kindness . . . love.'*[20]

As Paul wrote to Titus, *'He saved us, not because of righteous things we have done, but because of his mercy. He saved us through the washing of rebirth and renewal by the Holy Spirit.'*[21] Or as he wrote to the believers in Thessalonica, *'From the beginning God chose you to be saved through the sanctifying work of the Spirit and by belief in the truth.'*[22]

Jesus explained the consistent presence of the Holy Spirit in our lives by using a gardening simile: *'"I am the real vine and my Father is the vine-dresser. . . . It is essential that you should remain in me, and I in you. No branch can bear fruit in isolation by itself; it must remain in the vine. Just so, neither can you, unless you remain in me. I am the vine; you are the branches. If anyone remains in me, and I in him, he bears much fruit, because apart from me it is impossible for you to do anything. If anyone does not remain in me, he is thrown out like a withered branch. . . . When the Helper, whom I will send to you from the Father, comes, I mean the*

Spirit of truth . . . he will be a witness for me . . . . When he has come . . . he will convict the world of its own sin . . . he will guide you into all the truth.'' [23]

The great encouragement of the Christian Gospel is that the whole Godhead is on our side, and that even when we do not know how to approach God or what to say to Him in our prayers, *'the Spirit himself intercedes for us with groans that words cannot express. And he who searches our hearts knows the mind of the Spirit, because the Spirit intercedes for the saints in accordance with God's will.'* [24]

I wish I could take you to visit Stanislaw to see a living demonstration of the way the Holy Spirit transforms human lives. Such a visit is impossible because Stanislaw is serving out the remainder of his natural life on a prison sentence for a series of violent crimes. I have not spoken to him personally because he cannot speak English, but I have seen him and listened through an interpreter to his story.

My introduction to Stanislaw was unexpected. Pastor Paddy Boyle and I were guest speakers at a Christian family camp meeting in Poland in 1990. I was taking the morning youth spot and Paddy was taking the evening evangelism meeting. As I came down from the platform on the Tuesday morning, I became aware that our host had remained there and was making some kind of special announcement and appeal. Suddenly the 850 or so who had assembled in the marquee for the youth meeting turned together in twos and threes and began praying. Someone noticed that Paddy and I had not caught on to the significance of these prayer-huddles, so he came over to explain.

The prayer was on behalf of seven prisoners who had submitted a request to their prison governor that they be allowed to visit the camp. This was the result of the work of a pastor who had begun visiting the prison some years previously. Gradually indifference and mockery turned to interest, and prisoners began to turn up in large numbers to his meetings. He would spend time talking to the group and also individual time with each prisoner. More than a dozen of the convicts had warmed to the Christian Gospel and had expressed a wish to be baptized and become Christians. This included the seven who were now asking for the privilege to be released to the custody of the pastor so that they might attend our camp.

The problem was that these men all had violent histories, and most were serving sentences for murder or assault. Early reports suggested that the Governor was going to decline the request on that basis. The special prayer was to ask the Lord to prevail upon the Governor to allow these men to have temporary freedom. Next day Paddy and I were returning to the campsite when we heard that a special meeting had convened in the marquee. When we walked in, the whole tent was buzzing with excitement. Six of the seven men were there on the platform, being introduced by their pastor. It was an absolutely amazing experience as one after the other gave his testimony.

When Stanislaw stood to speak, his frame bore the marks of a violent man. He had an intimidating physique, and his face exhibited a tough life, but he spoke a different kind of passion. There was no violence in his voice, and he did not wish to specify his crimes, except to suggest that by his hands more than one innocent person had died. He had been sentenced to life, and had vowed as he was frog-marched protesting into prison that he would escape at the earliest opportunity. He kept his word and escaped a few weeks later.

For the next seven years Stanislaw lived rough in the forest. No one knew he was there, and he lived as instinct told him how best to survive, sometimes trapping game, sometimes raiding homes and farms for food. Then one day he was discovered and returned to a high-security prison. He had been confined there for seven more years when the pastor came preaching. At first Stanislaw spurned every invitation to participate and scorned those who did, but in time the Spirit softened him and he went along to see what was on offer. He found a pastor who would listen to him and who seemed genuinely concerned for his well-being, and he found the offer of forgiveness and a new life in Christ.

I shall never forget that Saturday afternoon by the Baltic Sea as Stanislaw and his five fellow-convicts entered the sea to be baptized, the first of about sixty people immersed that day. As he surfaced from the baptism he punched the air in ecstatic delight, then took a bottle and filled it with Baltic water, not as a keepsake but for the seventh prisoner, who had not been permitted temporary freedom but who nonetheless wished to be associated with his colleagues in the baptism. The water would be emptied into the contents of a specially-erected baptismal tank at the prison so that he could at least imagine that it was the Baltic!

The next day Stanislaw and his friends boarded their bus and returned without resistance to their prison. At no time had they been restrained physically; there had been no guards with them, no handcuffs, not even any plain clothes policemen. They had been released on trust to the custody of the pastor, such was the confidence that the Governor had in his word and in their transformation. It was the strangest and strongest testimony I have ever witnessed of the working of the Holy Spirit. Violent men whom you could not trust for a moment had been transformed to trustworthy gentle men of their word.

Back in John's letter to Gaius, we come across Diotrephes, who appears to have been bad news for the local church. We must return to consider his case in the next chapter. Meanwhile, *''If anyone remains in me . . . he bears much fruit.''* [25] Gaius was a goodie, and that's how!

---

[1]2 John 7. [2]2 John 7, 9. [3]1 John 1:5-7. [4]Galatians 5:25 (Barclay). [5]3 John 9ff. [6]Ezekiel 36:25ff. [7]Exodus 30:19. [8]Leviticus 14:51. [9]Numbers 19:18. [10]Zechariah 13:1. [11]Matthew 3:6. [12]Exodus 7:13, 22, etc. [13]See Jeremiah 17:9. [14]See Ezekiel 36:26. [15]John 3:3ff (Barclay). [16]Matthew 16:16. [17]John 3:3, 8. [18]1 Corinthians 12:3. [19]Galatians 5:22ff. [20]2 Peter 1:5ff. [21]Titus 3:5. [22]2 Thessalonians 2:13. [23]Selected from John 15 and John 16 (Barclay). [24]Romans 8:26ff. [25]John 15:5 (Barclay).

When is a Christian not a Christian?

DOES THE NAME Gordon Wilson mean anything to you?

There is more than one Gordon Wilson, of course, but the one I wish you to recall is that dignified and gracious Christian Ulster man we saw in the media following the murder of his daughter Marie at the Remembrance Day service at Enniskillen in 1987. His words of forgiveness provoked the admiration of the world. He bore no malice. He sought no revenge. He did not excuse, but nor did he accuse. He simply extended forgiveness.

He had authority to forgive, because he was a victim. No one is more truly a victim than a parent or a spouse. You could say he had primary authority to forgive because he was a primary victim. The people of Enniskillen, indeed of the Province, were victims, too. Their community had been violated. You could say that made them secondary victims. On that basis, they also had authority to forgive. Their will to forgive was enabled by the dignified example of Mr Wilson. If he could forgive, given the deep personal grief he had suffered, surely the community might find it in themselves to forgive as well.

In the same year — 1987 — Myra Hindley signalled British society that she wanted forgiveness, too. Hindley had been convicted in 1966 for her part with Ian Brady in the sordid murder of five children. Hindley's part was to lure the children, Brady's was to torture and to kill. Together they buried the bodies on the moors. Hindley was chillingly impassive and unremorseful at the trial.

During her subsequent sentence in prison, it is said she returned to the Catholic faith of her childhood. Perhaps that influenced her, after twenty-one years of denying all knowledge, to volunteer to help the police in 1987 to try to locate the graves of Pauline Reade and Keith Bennett, though the search proved unsuccessful. Was this concession conclusive proof of her repentance, or a cynical gesture aimed at gaining her release from prison? We do not know.

In December 1994, Gordon Wilson was in the news again following a second family tragedy, the death of his only son Peter in a motoring accident. Again, dignity and Christian faith were calmly evident in spite of the depth of the loss and the double twist of the knife of pain.

Coincidentally in the same week, Myra Hindley stated her request for release from prison. She was quoted as saying: 'Words are inadequate to express my deep sorrow and remorse for the crimes I have committed and the pain they have caused. After thirty years in prison I think I have paid my debt to society and atoned for my crime. I ask people to judge me as I am now and not as I was then.'

In the Brady/Hindley case, you and I are secondary victims because our society was violated. She acknowledged that by her words 'paid my debt to society'. The primary victims were the parents and families of the murdered children. They have primary authority to forgive, but most cannot bring themselves to do so. We have only secondary authority but passions run deeply even now. There remains an instinctive feeling that, for some, a life sentence must mean life and not just a number of years.

Sinn Fein were also in the news in December '94. They demanded that those who murdered Marie Wilson (and hundreds of other innocent victims these past twenty-five years) had to be released because their actions were not 'crimes' but 'acts of war'. They suggested no remorse. They sought not to be forgiven but to be excused. They claimed their actions were justified. We retained a sneaking fear that if they did not surrender their arms, they might sooner or later resume their violence!

I do not wish to enter the political debate surrounding either case. I wish to raise the spiritual matter of repentance, forgiveness and (especially) tolerance.

When it comes to personal repentance, we must acknowledge that there is *no* excuse for the wrong we have done. 'It is not possible to explain the origin of sin so as to give a reason for its existence. . . . to excuse it is to defend it. Could excuse for it be found . . . it would cease to be sin.'[1] Humanity has been adept since Eden at coming up with excuses for sin, but that won't wash! Coming to the decision that we shall not maintain pretence, that we shall desist from wearing any mask when we approach God for forgiveness, means that we have agreed not to try to excuse what we have done or justify the kind of person we are. No more excuses! We are what we are. We are who we are. We admit that, we say sorry for that, and we are welcomed by God on that basis.

In the process, we effectively acknowledge that God is the primary victim of the sin of Lucifer and the sin of mankind. No one is more truly a victim than a parent. The rest of God's unfallen creation are secondary victims. At most, we the fallen world are tertiary victims. In spite of that, God bears no malice. He seeks no revenge. He does not excuse, but nor does He accuse. He simply extends forgiveness.

Therefore we should habitually recall the imperative that, though God accepts us as we are, He has absolutely no intention of leaving us as we are. He forgives but He also cleanses. He has more than a sneaking suspicion we cannot be trusted to retain our arms. We have no basis upon which to excuse or justify ourselves, or to try to hang on to our arms, our deficiencies or our warped characteristics. What is called for is complete and lifelong surrender.

As God implements the process of forgiveness and cleansing, we should habitually recall the expectation that as we seek forgiveness from God, so we must extend forgiveness to our fellow humans. We have no right to expect mercy from the primary victim while we deny it as a tertiary victim. When Jesus taught His disciples the Lord's Prayer, he included the line: ''''*Forgive us the wrongs we have done, as we forgive the wrongs that others have done to us.*'''' Then he added, '''*If you do not forgive others, then your Father will not forgive the wrongs you have done.*'''[2]

It is within this context that we may now consider the case of Diotrephes, which we have carried over from the previous chapter.

What of Diotrephes? How come he was such a pain in the neck in Gaius' church? Why wasn't he manifesting the same transforming grace of the Holy Spirit seen in Gaius? Why was he so belligerent and domineering, to the point of evicting from the church any who extended hospitality to the itinerant preachers? John said of Diotrephes he *'loves to be first'*, *'gossips maliciously about'* the church leaders, *'refuses to welcome'* those wandering evangelists, and even *'stops those who want to do so and puts them out of the church'.*[3] Not a nice man on the face of it. Indeed, it appears that he was just the kind of person who occasionally blights churches even today, whom you would think the church could well do without! It must have been a temptation to evict him from the group instead. After all, why should they tolerate such an arrogant man? Well let us not jump to conclusions, because his case is also, in its way, an ideal demonstration of the work of the Holy Spirit, which is both patient and potentially successful in every case.

Allow me a small detour by way of an illustration. I have used it to teach children.

I have a box of half-a-dozen bottles, all of them milk bottles except for one old-fashioned Coke bottle. The children are invited to withdraw one bottle at a time and to identify what they have found. On one occasion I used the talk with some children in Northern Ireland. A young man strode forward and pulled out the first bottle. 'It's a milk bottle,' he said. 'How do you know?' 'By its shape. We get milk in bottles this shape.'

In due course all the bottles are displayed, but they are not all the same shape, some being of the taller, older design, and some having advertisements printed on them for products such as Kellogg's Corn Flakes, or Legoland in Denmark. Naturally, they identify the Coke bottle by its different shape and by the 'Coke' registered trademarks. I also point out to them a message cast into the glass of a milk bottle during manufacture which reads: 'This bottle remains the property of the *** Dairy. Please rinse and return it for further use.' There is no similar message on the Coke bottle, because that company does not reuse them. They used to have an opposite message, 'No Deposit — No Return', but I think in recent years they have eliminated that message because it is not very 'green'.

I usually ask the whole group, 'Which of these two

bottles, the milk bottle or the Coke bottle, best represents the Christian?' They commonly opt for the milk bottle because they associate it with goodness. It is possible then to contrast the 'disposable' attitude of the hedonist with the 'Rinse and return for further use' attitude of the Christian, reinforced by the introduction of two Bible passages:

'Many live as enemies of the cross of Christ. Their destiny is destruction, their god is their stomach, and their glory is in their shame. Their mind is on earthly things.'[4]

'Do you not know that your body is a temple of the Holy Spirit, who is in you . . . ? You are not your own; you were bought at a price.'[5]

The pertinence of the object lesson is for adults as well as children. When God created human beings, He had big things in mind for us. Sadly, the majority do not care much for God and cannot be bothered with being Christians. They think it is boring. They have a 'Coke bottle' mentality. Their mind is only on earthly things, and in consequence at the end of the day they will be of no further use to anyone. Their destiny is destruction.

For the sincerely religious person, 'This life remains the property of God; please rinse and return for further use.' The Apostle John, Gaius, Demetrius, and even Diotrephes, were all examples of this latter group.

But there are some people who, though Christians, seem to give off a different message, just as milk bottles do which are not of the standard profile or which carry advertisements for various other commercial interests. They do things you do not expect good Christians to do. This may be because they make mistakes or commit sins unintentionally. Or it may be they commit sins because they have not yet asked God to change their lives. We do not need to judge them, but we do need to pray for them still. Because we may be perceived as one of them by neighbouring Christians. In other words, it is just as likely we are a Diotrephes as it is that we are a Gaius!

If we ask 'How can a Coke bottle be converted into a milk bottle?' we are asking 'How can a worldly-minded person become a Godly-minded person?' If we ask 'How can we overcome the problem among Christians that some do not behave according to our expectations of a good Christian?' we are asking 'How can we change a Diotrephes into a Gaius?' The answer is the same for both questions.

Were we strong enough, we might be able to squeeze a Coke bottle until it has the same shape as a milk bottle. But we have repeatedly noticed that human efforts to conform, by stopping doing all the bad things and attempting to do all the good things, fails to make one into a Christian. We would also be making the mistake of thinking we could recognize a good Christian by his outward shape, by his performance, or by his compliance with certain rules.

Is it too simplistic to suggest that if we took a Coke bottle just as it is, and poured some milk into it, it would immediately become a bottle of milk? It doesn't matter about the shape because the revised contents would allow that definition. There is a fine distinction between calling something 'a bottle of milk' and calling it 'a milk bottle'. There is a similar distinction between being classified a 'Christian' and being recognized as 'Christ-like'. Not all Christians are Christ-like — yet! The miracle is that as soon as human beings open themselves to the benefits and influence of Christ, they can rightly be identified as Christians. As they keep going back to be filled with that milk, gradually they are changed and one day they also more truly present the profile of the original. They live lives that can be seen to be fully Christ-like as well as Christian.

Peter wrote it this way: *'As newly-born children want nothing but their mother's milk, so you must set your heart on the pure milk that flows from the word of God, for it is by it that you will grow up in a steady progress towards salvation.'*[6]

I hope the model illustrates that the work of the Holy Spirit in transforming a life is not always an overnight success. On the face of it, our lives may continue to give confusing messages that appear to deny what we claim is happening from within. Sometimes that takes time, because the Spirit can deal only with those elements that we relinquish to Him. It is very easy to be blind to your own faults and to fail to renounce them. Remember Jesus' words for those who balked at the speck of dust in the eye of another while maintaining blissful ignorance of their own beam. So we turn again to 1 John 1:9 and the constant, unremitting need we have to approach God with confession on our lips.

Diotrephes was in the right place. He might have started into Christianity from a Coke bottle position; life a total denial of God, destiny destruction. He had become a receiver of milk, but his life retained some confusing messages that seemed to deny the presence or influence of Christ. But he was in the church, and that was vital. It is no good condemning him or putting him out. He needs encouragement and prayer so that he may discover his need and take it to the Lord in prayer.

Diotrephes also needs you and me in the church alongside him. And whatever we do we must avoid giving him the impression that 'God accepts me just as I am and He will accept you just as I am too'. God accepts Diotrephes where Diotrephes is, not where I am! That was a lesson the early church had to learn very soon, as you will see from Acts 11. No, it is not for anyone to discourage Diotrephes in that way. It will be the work of a careful pastor or experienced Christian working at the disposal of the Holy Spirit, to approach Diotrephes and gently suggest some changes in his disposition, while reassuring him that he remains God's child even now.

If NASA launched a new *Voyager* spacecraft with the objective of another moon landing, and then found that the on-board computer had put it into the wrong trajectory, they would attempt to save the mission from its present position. They would not bring it back to Cape Kennedy to start all over again. Within moments, a new course would be plotted by their computers, and the right moment would be calculated to make adjustments. There would be an optimum moment at which to blast the engines to bring about that change. Too soon or too late, and the mission could be entirely lost.

When God undertakes the mission of correcting our course, He takes us from the point where He finds us. Where He finds me is likely to be different from where He may find you. So, although our destination is the same, our course is different. From where I am it may look as though you're all wrong, or vice versa. Let's assume that God knows what He is doing and not be critical.

Gaius got it right. So did Stanislaw. Diotrephes got it nearly right. You and I get it right some of the time. We could get it right the whole time *if only* we would submit to the influence and working of the Holy Spirit and learn to march in step with Him, neither lagging behind reluctantly nor forging ahead on our own agenda. We must be *'born from above, of water and the Spirit'*. That will necessarily include the gift from God of being able to tolerate and forgive other individuals around us, even when they are a thorn in our flesh.

I could hardly end this chapter without asking again, *'Have you got the bottle to be a Christian?'*

---

¹*The Great Controversy*, pages 492, 493. ²Matthew 6:12, 14 (Good News Bible). ³3 John 9, 10. ⁴Philippians 3:18, 19. ⁵1 Corinthians 6:19, 20. ⁶1 Peter 2:2 (Barclay).

As true as the needle to the pole

IMAGINE A PASTOR. Imagine a senior man nearing the end of his years of ministry, perhaps aged just about 50, for that was the age when many pastors retired in his day. Life expectancy was possibly not much more.

The pastor I want you to imagine was a sincere man of God, a member of what was known as the 'believing remnant' — those who looked for the redemption of the world by the arrival of the Messiah. He believed, preached and taught that the Lord was coming soon. So far as he was concerned, Scripture irresistibly indicated the coming Messiah; the time prophecies relating to the 'Coming' appeared to expire in his day attesting that the time was near; the signs in the world about him seemed to scream out that the time was *now!*

He and his wife are described as *'godly folk, careful to obey all of God's laws in spirit as well as in letter.'* His wife, of similar age, was a good support in his ministry and a woman of prayer. They had no children, so their time was concentrated on the work of his pastorate.

Then imagine the household when the pastor comes home from his day's visiting and asks his wife, 'Elizabeth, could I ask you to prepare my things for next week? I have to go away to HQ for my turn of duty, and I want my robes and clothes to be cleaned and ironed.' He is not going to a synod meeting, nor a camp meeting; not a national Church committee, nor any similar convocation. He is going to Jerusalem! For our pastor is none other than *Zacharias*, the priest of a village in the hill country of Judaea, whose duties called him twice each year to travel to Jerusalem when his division of the priesthood took their turn of service at the temple.

Now imagine the subdued tension and anticipation each morning at dawn in the temple courtyard as the duty division of priests muster before the high priest. Responsibilities for the day are to be divided out randomly among the priests. These would include some of the most revered tasks, provoking a spirit of excited anticipation mingled with fearful trepidation, because some would be asked to enter the first section of the inner temple, the holy place. This was a huge privilege that might come to a priest only once in a lifetime, yet with the attendant threat of death if he were to offend God.

Lots were cast for the various duties of the day, the process going something like this. The priests would assemble in a semicircle around the high priest who would nominate certain numbers — let us hypothesize number 16, number 33, number 52 and number 75. That done, the priests would number-off from a point indicated by the high priest. Since no one could anticipate what numbers the high priest would call, nor what number he would be given, because he did not know from which point round the semicircle the high priest would begin the numbering-off, the whole process was unpredictable.

As the numbering proceeds, priest number 16 steps forward, and then the priest who finds himself numbered 33 also stands forward. As the numbering approaches Zacharias, he becomes conscious that the number 52 may fall to him. It does. He steps forward humbly, and the priests continue numbering off until all the numbered priests have been identified.

The assignments are varied, the first going to that priest who happened to be numbered 16. He must enter the holy place and clear the previous day's ashes from the altar of incense, before setting new burning coals on it that he has carried from the altar of burnt offering outside the front door. The second assignment goes to priest No. 33, who must make the sacrifice of the lamb by slaying the animal when the appointed hour strikes. Being the third priest nominated, Zacharias' role is to enter the holy place with incense, sprinkling some upon the burning coals so that the vapour rises and fills both the holy place and the most holy second portion of the temple, since the veil that separates the two sections does not reach fully to the ceiling. The rising vapour symbolizes the rising prayers of the people, the priest simultaneously chanting prayers seeking forgiveness for the nation and asking for the coming of Messiah. The fourth assignment is completed by our hypothetical priest No. 75, whose task is to complete the service by burning the carcass of the lamb on the altar of sacrifice.

Zacharias has the most onerous task, because if either the sacrificed offering or his own spiritual attitude as the officiating priest is unacceptable to God for any reason, it can result in his instant death. This means that the duty priest must first confess and repent of his own sin before he takes upon himself the duty of representing the people. According to Jewish tradition,[2] if the offering was not acceptable and God meant to kill the priest, there would be 'an appearance' to the right of the altar of incense.

Now imagine the terror that must have shuddered through Zacharias when such a manifestation appeared. *'A great crowd stood outside in the Temple court, praying as they always did during that part of the service when the incense was being burned. Zacharias was in the sanctuary when suddenly an angel appeared, standing to the right of the altar of incense. Zacharias was startled and terrified.'*[3] Talk about understatement! It was enough to cause death by heart failure.

But the angel reassured him, *'"Don't be afraid, Zacharias! For I have come to tell you that God has heard your prayer* (that is, his domestic petition, not the prayer now offered corporately for Israel), *and your wife Elizabeth will bear you a son. And you are to name him John. . . . He will be one of the Lord's great men. . . . and he will be filled with the Holy Spirit, even from before his birth. And he will persuade many a Jew to turn to the Lord his God."'*[4]

Imagine his relief! He was not to be struck dead. Instead, the dreams and prayers of the godly couple were fulfilled, and they were promised a son.

But he was struck dumb, because he muttered his doubts that the angel was right, by challenging *'"How can I be sure of this? I am an old man and my wife is well on in years."'*[5] God therefore chastised him by striking him dumb, in order to deepen his faith. It was only at the dedication of the baby that he was enabled to speak again.

Zacharias was a righteous man with a deficient faith. It is not uncommon to find the two together in the human experience, and that may cause us some encouragement. Apparently God's chastisement had the desired effect, because at the circumcision ceremony when John was named, Zacharias' tongue was freed and his first words were a blessing to God. He was filled with the Holy Spirit and gave this prophecy: *'"Praise the Lord, the God of Israel, for he has come to visit his people and has redeemed them. He is sending us a Mighty Saviour from the royal line of his servant David, just as he promised through his holy prophets long ago. . . . And you, my little son, shall be called the prophet of the glorious God, for you will prepare the way for the Messiah. You will tell his people how to find salvation through forgiveness of their sins."'* His son was none other than John the Baptist.

If I were to ask you who was the oldest man ever to live, and you were familiar with your Bible, you would probably say Methuselah. But you would be wrong. At the age of 969 Methuselah was buried! That makes him the oldest man who ever died. The oldest man who ever lived is Enoch, because he did not die. He *'walked with God; then he was no more, because God took him away.'*

If I were to ask you who was the greatest man who ever lived, you might say Jesus, and that would be understandable. But Jesus declared, *'"Among those born of women there has not risen anyone greater than John the Baptist."'*

However, life was not to be a bed of roses for John. His was to be a rigorous education, and his instructor was the Holy Spirit, who led him far away from the established rabbinical schools to the isolation of the desert so that his vision would be maintained untainted. *'The little boy greatly loved God and when he grew up he lived out in the lonely wilderness until he began his public ministry to Israel.'*

God had called the son of Zacharias to the greatest task ever committed to men. In order to accomplish that objective, to give new direction to the thoughts of the people and impress them with God's requirement of holiness, he must himself have a sound physical constitution, and mental and spiritual integrity. Therefore he must learn control of his own passions and natural appetite so that he could not be bought or sold by any social pressure or circumstance, even by the threat of imprisonment or death.

God achieved this by a number of measures. His Holy Spirit dwelt within John even before he was born, right through childhood and on through his ministry. This ensured that John's heart never became a hard and resistant sample of humanity, but remained supple and responsive to the Spirit, always willing to *'march in step with the Spirit'.*[10] God took him away from distracting and misleading official centres of learning and immersed him in uncompromised study of the Scriptures.

God also strictly moderated John's diet so that no dependency, excess nor impurity could corrupt his mind or clarity of thinking. There were four species of locusts that were declared *kosher*. Bedouins and Jews of the Yemen eat them still. 'Wild honey' is that of wild bees. By limiting John's diet in that way, God took him outside the normal economic framework of the country so that he could be liberated from bondage to a life-style and economy that blights most of us, so that he could be wholly devoted to his prophetic work. He had no need to work to earn a living, because his living was free. John was never to drink wine or other liquor.[11] Like Samson, John was to be a Nazarite, dedicated to God in the special way outlined in Numbers 6.

By taking him through such a rigorous life-style, God prepared John to weather subsequent hardship and deprivation without wavering. The result was a man who could not be bought or sold, a man who in his inmost soul was true and honest, who did not fear to call sin by its right name, and whose conscience was as true to duty 'as the needle to the pole'.[12] He would stand for the right even though the world might fall about his ears.

John's commission was to *'"turn the hearts of the fathers to their children and the disobedient to the wisdom of the righteous — to make ready a people prepared for the Lord."'*[13] His training at the hands of the Holy Spirit resulted in a direct and unequivocal message, *'"Repent, for the Kingdom of God is almost here."'*[14] Consequently, a continuous stream of people flocked from Jerusalem, from all over

Judaea and from all over the Jordan valley, to hear him and to be baptized in the River Jordan.

The purpose of this present chapter is firstly to examine that message, and secondly to notice the example John is to those of us living today who desire to be a Christian, who are also called to 'prepare a people for the Lord'.

'Repent!' is another way of saying 'Turn from your sins to God'. The Greek word means 'change your mind, have a complete change of heart', while the underlying Hebrew concept is 'turning, returning' which means turning from one's sins and returning to God. Notice that there is not only a 'from' but a 'to', because turning from one's sin is impossible unless at the same time one turns to God — otherwise the effect is merely to turn from one set of sins to another.

'The Jewish understanding of repentance is that each individual must do it, yet it requires God's grace to be able to do it. "Turn us to you, O Adonai, and we will be turned" (Lamentations 5:21).'[15]

John was inviting them to respond to the same prophetic promises we have noted in earlier chapters, especially from Jeremiah and Ezekiel, '"I will sprinkle clean water on you, ... I will give you a new heart and put a new spirit in you; ... I will save you from all your uncleanness."'[16] His hearers probably recognized this intended connection, and on the whole responded gladly, dilettante Pharisees and Sadducees proving the exception.

As Dr David Stern points out, John's appeal was not the ranting of 'an overwrought, undereducated charlatan yelling at a frightened and equally illiterate crowd'. The urgency to 'Repent' was reasoned on the basis that *'The Kingdom of God is near!'* This 'refers neither to a place nor to a time, but to a condition in which the rulership of God is acknowledged by humankind, a condition in which God's promises of a restored universe free from sin and death are, or begin to be, fulfilled.'[17]

John was offering the people a new context for the old practice of ritual cleansing. The Jewish people were familiar with ritual cleansing by bathing in water, because one had to be ritually clean before entering the Tabernacle or Temple.

Ritual purity could be lost in a number of ways, the pre-eminent way of restoring it being through washing, as a study of Leviticus will show. Even today the use of a *mikveh*, or ritual bath, is practised by observant Jewish men and women. What John is offering is new, for it is cleansing not just from a momentary lapse but from a life pattern of sin.

Again it will be useful to note the way today's Messianic Jews understand John's message, because they may give us insights we twentieth-century Christians could otherwise miss. So back to Dr Stern who by defining confession from a Jewish perspective says it means to: ' "Agree, admit, acknowledge, declare publicly, confess", literally, "say the same thing". In the case of confessing one's sins, one is saying the same thing about them that God says, acknowledging the deeds to be wrong, willing to declare publicly one's sorrow, guilt and resolution to change.'

He continues, 'We live in an age when many people do not know what sin is. Sin is violation of *Torah* (1 John 3:4), transgression of the law God gave his people in order to help them live a life which would be in their own best interests as well as holy and pleasing to God. In the so-called Age of Enlightenment, two or three centuries ago, the notion of moral relativism began to gain a hold in Western societies. Under its sway people discarded the concept of sin as irrelevant. In this view there are no sins, only sicknesses, misfortunes, mistakes, or the outworking of one's environmental, hereditary and biological input (Western terminology) or of one's fate or karma (Eastern). Alternatively, sin is acknowledged to exist, but only as defined in one's culture. Cultural relativism thus negates the biblical concept of sin as absolute wrong.'[18]

John's message, and indeed much of the Bible, 'is concerned with explaining what sin is, what the penalty for sinning is, how we can avoid that penalty and have our sins forgiven, and how we can live a holy life free from the power of sin, pleasing to God and to ourselves.'[19] John was prepared to identify sin for what it is and was not prepared to excuse it as merely 'the outworking of one's environmental, hereditary and biological input'. This got him into trouble and eventually caused his death, but he was prepared even to address and specify the sins of the aristocracy if opportunity arose.[20]

He made it clear that the consequence of unrepented sin was unavoidably judgement, as in his rebuke to the Pharisees, *'"Brood of vipers! Who put it into your heads to flee from the coming wrath?"'*[21] But he also made a clear appeal to avoid such penalty by confession of sin and repentance. When asked by tax-collectors, soldiers, or the common man about specific advice to live a more holy life, he gave clear instruction which echoes the counsel of Jesus from the Sermon on the Mount.[22]

We may attempt a summary of John's message as follows: 'Turn from your sins; return to God; acknowledge His rulership; acknowledge that your life's deeds are sin; publicly declare your sorrow for that; be cleansed and liberated from a life pattern of sin; live free from the power of sin; be a part of the Kingdom of God!'

Surely John's message, so relevant to his contemporaries, is as relevant to you and me today and to our contemporaries! And I sincerely hope that the message of this book reflects the same relevance, and as effectively shows you 'what sin is, what the penalty for sinning is, how we can avoid that penalty and have our sins forgiven, and how we can live a holy life, free from the power of sin, pleasing to God and to ourselves.'

In concluding this chapter I would like to notice the example John is to you and me, who desire 'to be a Christian' and are also called to 'prepare a people for the Lord' before He returns.

'In preparing the way for Christ's first advent, (John) was a representative of those who are to prepare a people for our Lord's second coming. The world is given to self-indulgence. Errors and fables abound. Satan's snares for destroying souls are multiplied. . . . Self-discipline is essential to that mental strength and spiritual insight which will enable us to understand and to practise the sacred truths of God's word.'[23]

The challenge for you and me, then, is not just to settle for a status quo Christianity (if such a thing is really possible!), not to settle for a life which is little more than a slightly-modified version of the chicken syndrome, but to review our outlook entirely so that it encompasses the very highest standards of the Kingdom of God. If we will accept the discipline that John accepted, controlling our life-style and appetite and ensuring clear access to our minds for the Holy Spirit, then we, too, can be equipped for service,[24] as 'true as the needle to the pole'.

---

[1]Luke 1:6 (Living Bible). [2]Arnold Fruchtenbaum, *Life of Messiah From a Jewish Perspective*. [3]Luke 1:10 (Living Bible). [4]Luke 1:13ff (Living Bible). [5]Luke 1:18. [6]Luke 1:68ff (Living Bible). [7]Genesis 5:24. [8]Matthew 11:11. [9]Luke 1:80 (Living Bible). [10]Galatians 5:25 (Barclay). [11]Luke 1:15. [12]*Education*, page 57. [13]Luke 1:17. [14]Matthew 3:2 (Barclay). [15]*Jewish New Testament Commentary* (JNTC), page 16. [16]Ezekiel 36:25ff. [17]JNTC, page 16. [18]JNTC, page 17ff. [19]JNTC, page 18 *Serious readers would do well to obtain a copy of Dr Stern's *Commentary*, and particularly to study the fifteen pages of comment on Romans 5:12-21, which it is not possible to undertake here. [20]Luke 3:19, 20. [21]Luke 3:7 (Barclay). [22]Luke 3:10ff. [23]*The Desire of Ages*, page 101. [24]2 Timothy 3:16, 17.

Guard well the avenues of the soul

ANTON WAS A computer sales-executive-cum-consultant, whose work demanded that he spend a lot of time away from home. He was good at his job. He enjoyed his work, and, as well as earning a high salary he got tremendous satisfaction from the challenge of clinching the sale and from the benefits of the business social life that was part and parcel of his routine. Unfortunately, his appointments frequently invaded his domestic social life, because he did not get home until late in the evening, and often had to stay away in hotels because his sales territory was so extensive. However, he would try to compensate by inviting Beulah to any weekend functions that his career involved, and he jealously phoned her every day on the mobile phone he had specially bought for her, to see that she was all right.

Beulah was Anton's wife. She liked their up-market, richly furnished home and enjoyed the financial benefits of Anton's high income. She had every modern convenience possible to make housework light, and cable television to maximize the viewing options to while away the time. She did not like the enforced loneliness when Anton was away, but she didn't tell him that. Instead she started to find a life for herself in the community. She did not need the money but she took a part-time job in an architects' office to help fill the time, which brought an added bonus of a nice social life because many of the staff would play squash or badminton a couple of times a week. That was where she began to get to know Claude more intimately.

Claude, the senior partner in the company, was older than Beulah and Anton. He was a widower who had a nice home across the river on the other side of town, one of those really nice men who made people feel good about themselves because he listened well. He had a handsome physique and a kind face. He was so considerate that Beulah could not help warming to him. Occasionally, to begin with, the two of them would remain behind for a drink together when the badminton had finished, and that was when the chemistry started to happen. Before long they were going back to his place for a drink that became a little more than that if Beulah knew exactly what Anton's schedule was. Once Anton had made his daily phone call, she was free to return home at whatever hour she found convenient.

One day Claude took an early lunch and invited Beulah along. She could not entirely relax until Anton had phoned, and as the day wore on she wondered what had happened. Then she realized that the batteries on the mobile phone had gone flat, and that Anton would ring their home number instead. He was due home that day, but he had not said just when he expected to arrive. She started to panic, made her excuses with Claude and drove to the only traffic bridge across the river, thinking that she might just get home before Anton did, and then she could avoid any difficult questions. He was a very jealous husband.

When she got to the bridge, the police had a cordon across it and there was a traffic queue a mile long. Apparently a world-renowned terrorist called The Don had climbed onto the superstructure, armed with a bomb and a rifle, and was threatening to blow the bridge up if his organization did not receive £5m by sunset. He was also threatening to shoot anyone who tried to use the bridge meanwhile. Already a number of shots had been fired, though no one had been hit.

Beulah just could not wait until that time; it was going to be hard enough explaining her lateness home from work, let alone coming up with an excuse for being over the other side of the river in another suburb. She made for the ferry instead. Although it was slow and archaic, at least it was still operating down stream. But she had no cash for the ferry toll, so she called at her friend Evette's to ask her for a £1 coin.

Evette knew full well what Beulah and Claude were up to, and because she was a Christian she did not feel that she should encourage them in even the slightest way. When Beulah explained her need and the reason for the panic, Evette calmly said 'No', she would not give her even one penny, because that would make her an accomplice in the sordid affair.

Time was pressing, so Beulah headed for the ferry. She knew Fred the ferryman quite well because she had been that way several times over recent weeks, but when she asked him for credit, he said it was more than his job was worth. 'The firm might check up on me,' he said, 'and I can't afford to lose my job.'

Beulah was desperate, so she raced back to the bridge. It was still cordoned off, but by approaching from a different direction she could see that the cordon consisted only of a few cones across the road and a couple of policemen standing rather nervously looking towards The Don, so she decided to make a run for it. She blasted past the cones and the policemen and was well over the bridge when she heard the first shot. She decided to swerve from side to side of the road in an effort to avoid his bullets, but she was going so fast that she caught the kerb and the car was flicked over, bursting through the balustrade. Her car plunged into the river below which was in full tidal flow. Sadly, she was dead long before the divers managed to get near to rescue her.

At the inquest, everybody blamed the others for her death, each for different reasons. But who do you think was most responsible? Was it Anton because of his neglect and jealousy? Was it Beulah because of her lapse of morals and loyalty? Was she to blame for not confiding her loneliness and disappointment to her own husband, so that he could do something about it? Was it Claude for inviting (enticing?) her out for the afternoon? Should Anton have serviced the phone batteries better? Could not Evette or Fred have been more helpful, and were they not responsible in some way? And what about The Don; if he had not been there, shooting so wildly, there never would have been a risk!

The coroner recorded 'death by misadventure'. It was just bad luck! One of those things. It had not been murder, nor even manslaughter. It had not been suicide. No one was to blame because it was just a freak accident caused when Beulah's wheel caught the kerb. It could have happened in any number of circumstances.

No doubt Beulah would have claimed that had Anton showed her more concern in terms of actually being there in the evenings instead of getting so caught up in his career, she would never have been enticed away by Claude. If only he had not so jealously phoned each day, there would have been no panic.

Claude had his excuses too. It was the chemistry. It just happened. If anyone was to blame for the affair it was Anton. If anyone was to blame for the death, it was the so-called friend Evette, so pious it almost made him vomit. And for goodness' sake, what was Fred's job compared with Beulah's life! Surely he could have bent the rules just once!

When God asked Adam, *'"Have you eaten from the tree that I commanded you not to eat from?"'*, Adam said, *'"The woman you put here with me — she gave me some fruit from the tree, and I ate it."'* It must be God's fault for putting the woman there, or the woman's fault for enticing him. Surely it was not down to Adam!

Eve claimed, *'"The serpent deceived me."'* Surely it was Satan's fault, not hers! She was not to blame! Besides, the fruit looked nice, and no one died, anyway!

The pattern for sinners ever since Eden has been to blame everybody or everything else, or to make excuses in some other way. 'Who says it's a sin, anyway?'

When Satan tempted Jesus, he sought some small chink in Jesus' armour by which he could prise Him open altogether and cause His downfall. It is not unreasonable to want food, so why not use your powers to make some from the stones? When Jesus responded by quoting Scripture, Satan thought he could out-manoeuvre Jesus by using Scripture too. 'The Bible says you can jump because God will command his angels to lift you up in their hands.' Jesus was *'tempted in every way, just as we are — yet without sin.'*[2] He knew He would be responsible Himself for surrendering to or resisting sin, and He made no excuses.

Satan can never compel us to sin. He cannot control our minds, unless of course we surrender them first. *BUT* every sinful desire we cherish affords him a foothold, and each foothold potentially leads on to overwhelming defeat. That is why we need to 'guard well the avenues of the soul', which means protect ourselves so far as we are able from any influence or circumstance that may lead us to sin. 'Prevention is better than cure' is a sentence we have memorized and repeated since childhood. Never is this more true than in our decision to be a Christian.

We have earlier noted that we need to provide access to our minds for the Holy Spirit to work. We should also deny access in every way possible to temptation and to the tempter. The two goals may be achieved by the same action, if we will use reading of the Scripture as a vehicle for the Holy Spirit to speak to our minds. Jesus said, *'"No one can serve two masters."'* This applies clearly to the matter of growing more like Jesus and conquering the sin in our lives. As we acknowledge the Kingdom of God in our own life, and allow access to the Holy Spirit, God becomes our master and changes us from the core outwards, while we achieve a cordoning-off of the avenues to the soul. Except that we have more than a few traffic cones; we have attendant angels.

Therefore, *'You must be abstemious. You must be on the alert. Your enemy the Devil prowls around, like a roaring lion, looking for someone to devour. You must resist him with a rock-like faith.'*

In the early 1980s an intruder successfully made his way into Buckingham Palace. Within the grounds of the Palace, a Special Branch police officer stopped and challenged him. After all, it was night-time!

The intruder said he was from the Gas Board and was responding to an emergency call. When asked for ID, the only thing he could produce was a crow-bar with British Gas markings on it. On that basis the officer let him through. Rather embarrassing!

We are no less gullible! Every day we permit access to our minds and lives of a whole host of invasive influences designed to entice us into forgetting God. As one writer put it, 'The crisis is stealing gradually upon us. The sun shines in the heavens, passing over its usual round, and the heavens still declare the glory of God. Men are still eating and drinking, planting and building, marrying, and giving in marriage.

Merchants are still buying and selling. Men are jostling one against another, contending for the highest place. Pleasure lovers are still crowding into theatres, horse races, gambling halls. . . . Satan sees that his time is short. He has set all his agencies at work that men may be deceived, deluded, occupied and entranced, until the day of probation shall be ended, and the door of mercy forever shut.'[5]

'The god of this world has blinded minds with the result that they cannot see the light that has dawned on them.'[6]

One day some of the elders went to visit Ezekiel. Remember, they were all captives, living as refugees in Babylonia. The elders wanted to ask Ezekiel to pray for God's guidance on their behalf. God's response rather knocks the wind out of your lungs when you first notice it, because He sternly says *'''I will not let you enquire of me!''''*[7] Their query is not specified, but perhaps it can be deduced from the direct answer which God does eventually provide in spite of having said He would not let them enquire of Him. It appears they wanted Him to condone or at least turn a blind eye to their wish to have an image to represent Him.[8] God knew from experience that if His people entertained any notion of compromise with His commandments, the result was a total disregard for them.

As we noted before, *'These things happened to them as examples and were written down as warnings for us, on whom the fulfilment of the ages has come. So, if you think you are standing firm, be careful that you don't fall! No temptation has seized you except what is common to man. And God is faithful; he will not let you be tempted beyond what you can bear. But when you are tempted, he will also provide a way out so that you can stand up under it. Therefore, my dear friends, flee from idolatry.'*[9] To 'flee' means the same as to 'guard well' the avenues of the soul.

In a way similar to God's experience with the people who approached Ezekiel, He knows that every opportunity *we* encourage for temptation to be harboured or find lodging in our lives threatens our survival and threatens His sovereignty. *'If in his ordeal a man is tempted to sin, he must not say: "I am being tempted by God." God cannot be tempted by evil, nor does he ever tempt anyone else. Each man is tempted when he is seduced and enticed by his own desire. Then the next thing that happens is that this desire conceives and becomes the mother of sin. And then, when sin is full-grown, it spawns death.'*[10]

Our problem is that, although we're individuals desiring to follow Jesus and live fully Christian lives, we enjoy, even sometimes encourage, flirtation with temptation. We ignore the risk because we think flirting is not actually sinning, and so assume we get the excitement without the penalty. It is rather like playing spiritual Russian roulette. The perverted thrill is to place just one live round in the revolver barrel and leave five empty, then to spin the barrel so that we do not know whether the hammer will strike the bullet or an empty chamber, put the gun to our forehead and squeeze the trigger. We must learn to choose not to flirt with sin, to seal off access to our minds and lives so that there is less risk of the gun's going off in our hands and destroying our lives. We must learn to make deliberate decisions not to compromise God's *Torah*, for he gave those Ten Commandments to *'his people in order to help them live a life which would be in their own best interests as well as holy and pleasing to God'.*[11]

We must be aware of the tension that is inherent in our salvation-struggle. Joni Eareckson Tada has written: 'We have one foot on earth and the other in Heaven. We swallow the dirt and grime of humanity, yet "have tasted . . . the powers of the coming age" (Heb. 6:5). Wouldn't it be easier if, right now, God yanked our one foot out of the mud and firmly planted it alongside our other foot in Heaven? The justification-sanctification-glorification scenario would be less messy if the middle part could be dropped, wouldn't it?'[12]

She continues by confirming that God has purpose in the development that our struggles bring, and that we need not be subdued by them: 'If you're battling pride, lust, or temptation, you're in a better state than many who have grown numb to the struggle, stagnated in apathy or indifference. The very fact that the devil assaults you, targeting you as a threat, should fill your mind with hope. If being at peace with the world, the flesh, and the devil means being at enmity with God, then being at war with them must mean being at peace with God.'[13]

Recognizing that God brings purpose from our struggles is not to suggest we encourage those struggles by flirting with temptation. As we *'Make every effort to be holy'*, we make a number of deliberate, conscious decisions which we need to reinforce and restate each day. Among these decisions is the choice to surrender to God's way of salvation and to forsake what we have identified as the 'Babylonian Brownie Point' method. Another will be to encourage access to our minds by the Holy Spirit via Scripture reading, to enable Him to renew our minds, and to strengthen that process by our prayer life. In this chapter we are recognizing another deliberate choice, equally important, which is to 'Guard well the avenues of the soul'.

If you do not yet understand what this 'guarding' will involve, consider the following:

• How much time during any given day does the Holy Spirit have to access your mind, compared with the amount of time when the tempter has access? For example, how many minutes a day do you spend in devotional reading, and how much watching TV? If you are to guard your soul, then you may have some adjustments to make.

• Can you identify any activity in your life that is, in all honesty, an excuse to flirt with sin? Is there some version of a Claude or a Beulah in your life? If so, it is going to be well for you to put the revolver down and stop playing with a loaded gun.

• How many times have you repeated during The Lord's Prayer the words, *'And lead us not into temptation, but deliver us from evil'*? Do you suppose that these words might be Jesus' way of suggesting 'Help me guard the avenues of my soul'?

• For a really positive example of the guarded soul, research more fully the early life and preparation of John the Baptist. You will not choose to go into a monastery or become a desert hermit, but there are lessons applicable to twentieth-century life-styles.

Let's close the chapter with another spiritual conundrum, as posed by 17-year-old Steve: 'Up till about three years ago I thought people who took drugs were stupid. I still do if you're talking about junkies. But now I think drugs are just like anything else — if you abuse them they're bad; if you don't abuse them, they can be OK. I smoke a joint now and then, but not during school, or even every time there's a party. Just once in a while. It's not as bad as everyone says. My parents would kill me if they knew I had ever smoked pot before. But they're hypocrites; they drink and that's no different.'[14]

How do you feel about Steve's statement? If you agree with him, what would you add to his statement? If you disagree, why? How does his line of reasoning help you evaluate the theme of this chapter?

---

[1]Genesis 3:11. [2]Hebrews 4:15. [3]Matthew 6:24. [4]1 Peter 5:8, 9 (Barclay). [5]*The Desire of Ages*, page 636. [6]See 2 Corinthians 4:4, Barclay. [7]Ezekiel 20:3. [8]Ezekiel 20:32. [9]1 Corinthians 10:11ff. [10]James 1:13-15 (Barclay). [11]*Jewish New Testament Commentary*, page 17. [12]*Discipleship Journal*, No. 49. [13]Ibid. [14]The Anton and Beulah scenario was developed from an idea planted by *Tension Getters*, volume one, published by Youth Specialties (USA).

No more church, Miriam!

MIRIAM WAS STUDYING away from home. Home was near Finchley in North London, and college was at Nottingham. As with many students, accommodation for her first year was in halls of residence, and that was where she met Anna, Julia, and Julia's boy-friend Peter.

Halls of residence can be as lonely as life for a policeman in Trafalgar Square, surrounded by hundreds of people, yet no one is his friend. Miriam found it that way at first, but Anna and Julia were particularly friendly and uncomplicated, and Miriam soon got to know them quite well. They did not share the same lectures and were all reading different subjects, but their paths often crossed at some time during the morning or evening. It was Peter who first started talking about a party that was coming up soon, and the two girls thought Miriam might like to go with them. She agreed.

The party turned out unexpectedly for Miriam, because it was actually a squash meeting organized by the Christian Union. Fortunately, it was not too heavy, and discussion was not limited to just the Christian view. Miriam was Jewish by birth, though the Cohen family had not been particularly strong on synagogue attendance. She did not look upon herself as being especially religious at all. Not that she was hostile; more indifferent. On reflection she had enjoyed the fellowship of the CU squash meeting and when Peter and the girls told her they were going again, Miriam was glad of the invitation to join them. Apart from anything else, it gave her something to do on a Friday evening.

In time Miriam began to be captivated by the discussions that headed more and more onto the subject of the Messiah, and she found herself liking the sound of this man Jesus of Nazareth. It was therefore quite an obvious and simple step to go along to church with Anna when that particular invitation came along. She felt intimidated by the idea, but once there she found the place full of young students her age. There had been times of extremely moving praise and celebration on some occasions at the synagogue, but she also liked the songs and feeling of acceptance she experienced at the church.

Miriam had almost decided to become a Christian officially when she went home for the Christmas holiday, but she was taken by surprise at the strength of opposition to that idea when she mentioned it to her mother. Her dad was even more vociferous. She had thought that since they had not been very regular in attending the synagogue nor in keeping the festivals, except in a very fleeting way, they would not raise any strong objection. She could not have been more wrong. 'You imagine how the family will treat us when they hear about it,' Mr Cohen had scolded. 'We are Jewish and you must always remember that with pride. No more church, Miriam! I forbid it.' Mum was weeping, 'Please, Miriam, do not disgrace us. No more church!'

Miriam was fiercely loyal to her family and to her ethnic roots, but she had found such warm friendship from Anna, Julia and Peter, and had begun to find real answers to some of her life questions from the CU and from church. It caused her quite a lot of stress, trying to decide what she would do.

When Miriam knocked at her door, Anna was, of all things, just serving up some fresh bagels to Julia and Peter. How could they be enjoying such a thoroughly Jewish food when she had come to tell them about the news from home! Was it coincidence or some divine irony?

Anna hugged her when Miriam told them the ultimatum her dad had issued, and encouraged her, 'Don't let it distress you. You know Christians believe as Jews do that we should honour our parents. God must have some plan in all this. Perhaps the best thing is to respect your parents' wishes for the time being, and who knows, at some time in the future God may open the way for you to become a Christian without dishonouring them!'

'No way, Jose!' argued Peter. 'Jesus was very clear about standing up for our decisions. You can't take up the plough and then turn back. Choosing Jesus and accepting Him as Messiah may cause a division in your family, but there are more important issues at stake than that. You just stand by your decision, and your parents will just have to accept it. If they don't like it, you know you will always have a warm reception from your new Christian family!'

'Just hold tight, Pete,' Julia moderated. 'There is a simple way to resolve this without going to war! "Make love not war" is what this is all about. The fact is that Miriam is here and the Cohen family is down in London. The obvious answer is that Miriam just needs to keep her head down and be diplomatic. When she is here she can still come with us to CU and to church. She can join the Church as she planned. But when she goes home she just blends in with the family and keeps mum about it. Easy!'

Somehow those bagels turned into the least appetising sample Miriam had ever tasted. Every mouthful reminded her of how much she loved her mum and dad, yet loved Jesus too. As she walked back to her room, her mind was swimming. She was troubled especially by the way her three Christian friends had come up with alternate resolutions for the problem. Which was right? Maybe the Bible was just for silly mixed-up kids! By the time she next saw the trio, she was ready to tell them she had decided to pass on religion. It was not worth the bother.'

Meanwhile, Monica had been sitting on the back row at her church for the last couple of years. She was bored with it all, and she had found that if she sat on the back row she could slip out to the toilet halfway through the sermon, and if she played it right she could kill about five minutes that way. Monica and her brother Jim had been taken to First Church for as long as they could remember. Mum made sure they were up and ready each week, and they went because she insisted. Their dad, Mr Jones, didn't go with them very often. Really, he just went on special occasions to keep Mrs Jones quiet.

Monica was tired of First Church. She didn't get involved with the youth programme any more, and hadn't done so for more than a year. Nothing ever went on anyway, and the other youth in the group were boring. She decided she would rather spend time with her friends from school. Then she met Dave.

Dave went to church, but his church was different. The people were excited, and their youth group buzzed. Monica went along with Dave to his church, not because she was looking for a revival in her religious life, but because she didn't want to lose him as a boy-friend. But she immediately felt the difference at his church, and her flagging spiritual interest was awakened. It didn't bother her that some of their doctrines were different, because she felt the fellowship was far more vital — linked more than a little with her desire to keep Dave.

When Mrs Jones heard which church Monica was attending she got quite concerned. 'Look, Monica, they do not teach the truth. They have doctrinal errors that would make your grandmother turn in her grave if she knew you were going there. You be careful or you'll get caught up with them. Why not bring Dave to our church.'

'Leave the girl alone!' Mr Jones intervened. 'She is old enough to make up her own mind. Monica, you please yourself. Wherever you are happy is good enough for me. It doesn't matter which denomination you belong to because all roads lead to God.'

Monica realized that Dave's church did have some doctrines she didn't totally agree with, and yet she wondered about First Church. They might have been doctrinally accurate, but wow! What a boringly dead place! Dave's church had a great youth group. Monica decided she would settle for that.[2]

I am inclined to ask for your responses to these two stories. I would love to hear how you would grade those in Miriam's experience; who you think has come over the best and who the worst. I would be interested in hearing from buzz groups how they respond to Monica's situation, and who they think is right. That is the usual way I use these interactive devices, because they create interest and make possible a discussion about so many aspects of the Christian life. But since I am in my room writing, and you, sometime later, will be in your room reading, no such interaction is possible. So I will settle for drawing some conclusions myself that you may like to consider.

Long ago I came to the conclusion that too many people, especially young adults, give up Christianity because of church. Church doesn't address their needs, does not address the issues that face them day-to-day, and is generally boring or unsatisfying. The trouble is, when they throw that bath water out, they also throw out the baby!

Please do not misunderstand me, but there is so much more on offer to the Christian than just church. I believe in church, and I look forward to singing the hymns, worshipping God in prayer, listening to the reading of the Word and the preaching of the sermon, and I feel encouraged to listen to the testimony of other Christians and share fellowship with them. I agree with the Apostle that we should *'keep paying attention to one another, in order to spur each other on to love and good deeds, not neglecting our own congregational meetings, as some have made a practice of doing, but, rather, encouraging each other.'* But that is only a tiny part of my whole Christian experience.

Remember Anton in our last chapter? He telephoned Beulah every day, though mostly only for a moment or two. He tried his best to organize his schedule so that he could spend at least some part of every weekend with her. He felt that that was enough to remind her he loved her. Many people might commend him for that. Almost everybody treats God and his Christian faith precisely that way too! A few rushed moments by telephone (or prayer) and a little time each weekend if it is convenient and not too intrusive on other arrangements, is all God gets. There is just too much to do, too many other important things to include, to give Him much more than that.

Little wonder that church seems boring! Little wonder that people give up on church and give up on God. What with boring church and restrictive church standards, no wonder people leave by the back door. But it could be so much better and richer than that. The Christian life is dynamically full and exciting when you take it on as a full-time twenty-four-hours-a-day adventure. There is never a dull moment in the real cut and thrust of committed daily living with God in mind. Going to church then is icing on the cake, and TV or going down the pub or to the cinema is what becomes boring. Yawn, yawn, fancy settling for something so mundane when God has so much excitement on offer.

Take my son Nathan, for example. In the past twelve months his Christian adventure has taken him to Bosnia three times; he has been driving trucks of relief aid, once even to the point of becoming stranded in Sarajevo for several days. He has also taken a truck down to Albania, and has been driving an old double-decker bus round his local town on fund-and-food raising projects for Bosnia and Albania. Almost every day for the last six months has been brimful of work and adventure, sometimes mingled with a measure of hazard, too. After dropping into bed exhausted yet excited each day, churchgoing to him has become a thorough delight, especially when he is able to share with others the news of these adventures. Then, rather than 'No more church!', it becomes a matter of 'No! *MORE* church, Miriam!'

In contrast, when your Christian life is restricted (by your own choice) to a momentary whispered prayer-on-the-run and an hour in church at the weekend, it bears no relationship with the balance of your life, and obviously it is boring. Now don't tell me 'It's all very well for you, but I just do not have time in the day or week to do what Nathan has done.' We must each interpret and apply the full Kingdom of God within our own contexts, but ultimately it is a matter of priorities, and as God transforms our perspective on life and we see how totally irrelevant our busy lives here-and-now are in comparison to the long view of eternity, we can discover an exciting Christian experience which will be a continual high.

Miriam met the quandary familiar to many thousands of people over the centuries, in trying to decide how vital are the claims of Jesus of Nazareth compared with the natural bond to the family. The Apostle was addressing the same dilemma in Hebrew believers back in the earliest days of the church. They could see that Jesus was the expected Messiah, and they received Him personally into their lives, but then times got tough. The Romans were persecuting Jews in an horrific anti-semitic purge, so they were getting it from that direction. Simultaneously, the Jewish political leadership were urging their people to be proud and stand firm, and not corrupt their ethnicity or their faith by compromise. It was time to stand bravely, to be counted. Yet defectors to the Christian doctrine were being excluded from the Temple and from everything Jewish in their culture and treated as *persona non grata*, so they were getting it from that direction too.

Additionally, the huge expectation and anticipation of Jesus' return was looking thinner and thinner by the day. They had hoped so much, and they had accepted Him as the true Messiah, yet they were getting all that stick and there was no sign of His returning. Perhaps they had made a terrible mistake. Had they got it wrong? Was it all a delusion? So many of them were drifting out the back door of their congregations and re-identifying themselves as, or confirming their identity with, the Jewish people.

The Apostle had to write in terms that they would understand and with which they could identify their true Hebrew roots. So he wrote to them in Hebrews: *'Endure hardship as discipline; God is treating you as sons. . . . No discipline seems pleasant at the time, but painful. Later on, however, it produces a harvest of righteousness and peace for those who have been trained by it. Therefore, strengthen your feeble arms and weak knees! "Make level paths for your feet", so that the lame may not be disabled, but rather healed. Make every effort to live in peace with all men and to be holy; without holiness no one will see the Lord.'*[4]

A twentieth-century westerner would miss the cleverness of the appeal contained in these words from the Apostle, because he would not detect the subtle reference to a mighty moment in Israel's history when Elijah challenged the people and the priests of Baal, *' "How long will you waver between two opinions? If the Lord is God, follow him; but if Baal is God, follow him." '*[5] In the translation of the Hebrew Scriptures into Greek (known as the Septuagint) the verse reads *'How long do you go lame on both hams?'* (that is, the part behind the thigh and knee). So the expression used by the Apostle in Hebrews *'so that the lame may not be disabled'* is associated with Elijah's appeal *'How long do you go lame . . . ?'* Presumably the Hebrew Christian would recognize that subtle connection and realize the Apostle was making the same appeal.[6]

How long will *you* waver between two opinions? If God *is* God, then serve Him. It is a matter of whether you have the courage (the bottle) to be a Christian and to keep up with the pace God sets!

---

[1] and [2] Both scenarios are developed from an idea planted by *Tension Getters*, Volumes I and II, published by Youth Specialties (USA). [3] Hebrews 10:24, 25; (Quoted from Jewish New Testament). [4] Hebrews 12:7ff. [5] 1 Kings 18:21. [6] *Word Studies–Hebrews*, K. S. Wuest.

Reprise: the pathway to freedom

YOU'LL HARDLY BELIEVE this story, because it sounds too false, but I can assure you it is true.

We set the metronome ticking, and asked five volunteers to count, one at a time. The first methodically counted, 'One, two, three, four, five, six, eight, nine, ten, eleven.' Making no comment, we proceeded to the second candidate, asking him to count the strokes, and he did the same, arriving at eleven. The third repeated this pattern.

The fourth 'volunteer' was the only true volunteer, whereas the others had been hand-picked and briefed beforehand to count as they had, deliberately miscounting by omitting the number seven while sounding confident and assured that they had made no mistake. The congregation had been briefed, too, as to what we were doing, trying to coerce the fourth candidate to count the ten strokes of the metronome as if there were eleven. He obliged, and did not hesitate as he counted, 'One, two, three, four, five, six, eight, nine, ten, eleven.' The fifth volunteer counted as primed.

It was our Youth Day in East Anglia, and young people had travelled from many places to be with us. The theme was Freedom, and the illustration was designed simply to demonstrate how easily we succumb to peer or group pressure and willingly opt to conform to expectations rather than appear different or risk being deemed wrong, even though we feel sure inside that we are right.

When we owned up to the manipulated experiment, we asked our only true volunteer why he had chosen to repeat the mistakes of his colleague volunteers. He said, 'Because I was outnumbered. I thought there were only ten strokes each time, but they all counted eleven and you did not correct them, so I thought I must be missing something somewhere, so I went along with the rest.'

Jesus said, '"You are slaves to sin, every one of you. And slaves don't have rights, but the Son has every right there is. So if the Son sets you free, you will indeed be free."'[1] When He started His preaching ministry, Jesus knew that people

were in bondage, captivated by the most contemptible confidence trick launched on to God's people. Tragically Satan
was able to use the lips and indoctrination of the religious
leaders to pull it off. The Pharisees were 'an exemplary band
of teeth-gritters and finger-pointers',[2] meaning that they
viewed holiness as being achieved by gritting one's teeth in
self-discipline and pointing the finger at anyone of whom
they disapproved. So in Jesus' preaching ministry, we find
Him intent on breaking that yoke.

Jesus' central message was identical to that of John the
Baptist: '"Repent, for the kingdom of God is near."'[3] We
have previously summarized this message as inviting His
listener to 'Turn from your sins to God'. We noted 'in the
case of confessing one's sins, one is saying the same thing
about them as God says, acknowledging the deeds to be
wrong, willing to declare publicly one's sorrow, guilt and resolution to change'.[4]

Within days of Jesus' first proclamation of that theme,
He went on to explain how fundamentally different this
teaching was from the bondage that the Pharisees taught,
when He spoke the blessings, or beatitudes, recorded in
Matthew 5. He said, '"The thief comes with the sole intention of stealing and killing and destroying, but I came to
bring life, and far more life than before."'[5] We refer to those
teachings as Jesus' Sermon on the Mount.

Although I set out with no conscious intention to do so,
as I review the manuscript of this book I detect that I have
followed rather loosely the same sequence that Jesus outlined
on that hillside in Galilee. Therefore, perhaps a brief summary of Jesus' teaching on that occasion will confirm you in
your acceptance of those most important of messages, in
order that you may be 'free indeed' to live the Christian life
with delight, far more than before.

Jesus began, '"Blessed are the poor in spirit, for theirs is
the kingdom of heaven."'[6] Professor William Barclay has
translated these words, '"O the bliss of those who know their
need of God"'[7], or '"O the bliss of those who realize the
destitution of their own lives."'[8] This is the beginning of the
pathway to freedom. To be 'poor in spirit' means to recognize

and admit one's spiritual destitution, to face reality and acknowledge the bankruptcy in oneself, helpless unless God intervenes.

'The poor in spirit are blessed because they have come to the end of their efforts to make it on their own and, having failed, are no longer too proud to admit it. They are desperate.'[9] It is futile to seek to gain God's approval by solo human effort, or to attempt to win Brownie points to impress God. John Bunyan's case study, the illustration of the four chairs, and the later illustration of the milk bottles, were my way of saying, 'Blessed are the poor in spirit.'

Self-sufficiency is the subtlest serpent in earth's garden. Poverty of spirit is the end of denial, and the beginning of admitting to God the way we are. When the publican did that, he *went down to his house justified rather than the other*,[10] (that is, the proud Pharisee). The beginning of the pathway to Christian freedom is to acknowledge we are spiritually destitute, approaching God because of what He can do for us, rather than thinking we merit some reward for our own achievements.

Jesus continued, *'"Blessed are those who mourn, for they will be comforted."'* 'Mourning' in this context is the 'godly sorrow' of 2 Corinthians 7:10, which leads to repentance. From a broken heart it cries, 'O God, I have been hurt so much and I have hurt You and others so much in retaliation. Help me!' Mourning is grieving over my spiritual desperation.

'Meekness' is throwing yourself on God's mercy. It is an attitude that says, 'I have no hope but God for survival, so I will trust utterly in Him.' It means we give up expecting other people to meet our needs, give up trying to jump through their hoops to win approval, and relinquish ourselves to God, because His approval is all that matters. The meek know that only God can faithfully and constantly meet their physical, spiritual and emotional needs.

'Blessed are those who no longer hunger for people's respect, for attention, or even for the pain to go away. Blessed are they because, having found the true Bread and the living Water, they crave only that right relationship to

God that gives them access to these things. They thirst to see God's righteous will fulfilled in their lives and those of others.'[1]

The middle and later chapters of this book attempt to show how God knows every detail of our lives, and that knowing us so well He still loves us and wishes us only to return to Him, allowing access for the Holy Spirit into our lives to change us fundamentally from the inside outwards. A hunger and thirst for God and His righteousness can be nurtured and developed by allowing Him that access, and we can simultaneously starve to death our lust for the tempter's alternatives.

How blessed are those who are also merciful because, having recognized their own spiritual poverty, they can have compassion on others. We should not merely tolerate the 'Diotrephes' of this world, but live alongside them happily as we recognize that God accepts them just as they are, and as we grow towards God together.

'*"Blessed are the pure in heart, for they will see God"'*, Jesus continued. We noted that the heart is the core of the human, that habits of our lives are seated deeply at that core, and that we must welcome the Holy Spirit with His scalpel to perform radical heart surgery. The Word of God is that scalpel. The effect of that surgery is reinforced and enabled by prayer, and by making deliberate choices to guard the avenues to our souls, re-prioritizing our lives so that we are no longer trying to serve two masters.

As we break free from the bondage of Babylonian Brownie-point attempts at salvation, and our bottles are replenished by the milk of God's Word, so our perspective changes and our ambitions are raised. Then the delusion of this world stands out like a sore thumb, and we realize the majority are counting to eleven because they skip the important seven. The chicken syndrome is no longer for us! We have made the discovery that we have the face to be Christians — we do not require masks to hide behind.

---

[1]John 8:34-36 (Living Bible). [2]Karen Hinckley in 'A Fresh Look At The Beatitudes', *Discipleship Journal*, No 49. [3]Matthew 4:17. [4]See Chapter 9.

[5]John 10:10 (Phillips). [6]All of the Beatitudes are found in Matthew 5:3ff. [7]W. Barclay, *A Plain Man Looks At The Beatitudes*. [8]W. Barclay, *The New Testament*. [9]Karen Hinckley, op cit. [10]Luke 18:14, KJV. [11]Karen Hinckley, op cit.